THE ART OF Disney STRANGE WORLD

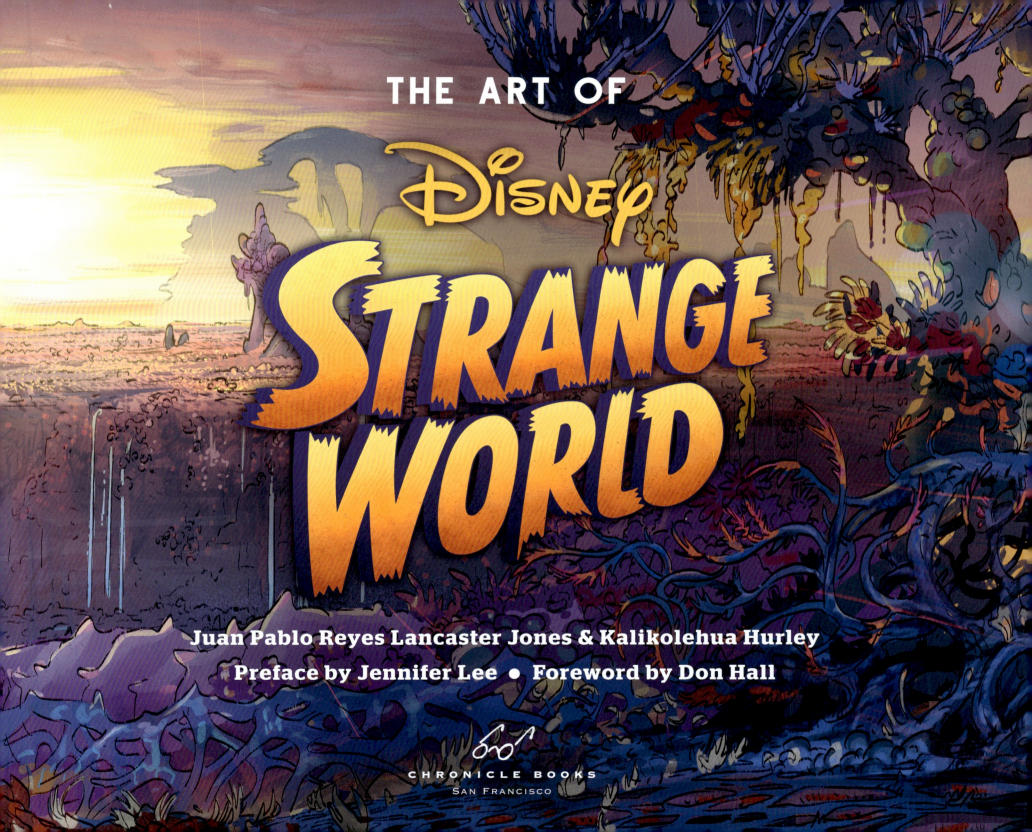

THE ART OF

Disney

STRANGE WORLD

Juan Pablo Reyes Lancaster Jones & Kalikolehua Hurley

Preface by Jennifer Lee ● Foreword by Don Hall

CHRONICLE BOOKS

SAN FRANCISCO

Creating a Walt Disney Animation Studios feature film involves years of inspired collaboration and the highest levels of artistry. Before the final rendered images of *Strange World* were seen on screens around the world, the following artists contributed their talents to the digital images included in this book:

Paul Aichele, Michael A. Altman, Camille Andre, Virgilio John Aquino, Manu Arenas, Laurie Au, Javier Ledesma Barbolla, Scott Beattie, Cameron Black, Marc Bryant, Brent Burley, Ian Butterfield, Jesus Canal, Gabby Capili, Angelo Sta Catalina, Juan Pablo Chen, Yolanda Cheng, Clio Chiang, Matt Jen-Yuan Chiang, Ramya Chidanand, Courtney Chun, Francois Coetzee, Justin Cram, Charles Cunningham-Scott, Alessandra Rodriguez Curiel, David G. Derrick Jr., Moe El-Ali, Craig Elliott, Logan Erdner, Jesse Erickson, Erik Eulen, Henrik Fält, Paul Felix, Ben Fiske, Julia "Fitzy" Fitzmaurice, Mike Gabriel, Leticia TR Gillett, Logan Gloor, Eric Goldberg, Ryan Green, Yasser Hamed, Mark Hammel, Juan E. Hernandez, Ki Jong Hong, Limei Hshieh, Wei-Feng Wayne Huang, Benjamin Min Huang, Eric Hutchison, Katherine Ipjian, Teny Aida Issakhanian, Mehrdad Isvandi, Sean D. Jenkins, Tyre Jones, Michael Kaschalk, Avneet Kaur, Mason Khoo, Jin Kim, SuZan Kim, Chaiwon Kim, Kate Kirby-O'Connell, Daniel Kole, Alex Kupershmidt, Ryan Lang, Brian Leach, Sang Jun Lee, Joyce Lee, Konrad Lightner, Yu-Tzu Lin, Dan Lipson, Kendall Litaker, April Liu, Shutong Liu, Alena Loftis, Cory Loftis, Luis Logam, Burny Mattinson, Brian Missey, Michael Morris, Adil Mustafabekov, Kevin Nelson, Nicholas Orsi, Allen Ostergar IV, Meg Park, Christoffer Pedersen, Zachary Angelica Petroc, Nick Putez, Liza Rhea, Mikki Rose, James Schauf, Armand Serrano, Justin Sklar, Amy Lawson Smeed, Ryan C. Smith, Jeff Snow, Jonathan Soto, Pamela Spertus, Michael W. Stieber, Lance Summers, David Suroviec, Marc Thyng, Timmy Tompkins, Lissa Treiman, Mary Twohig, Tadahiro Uesugi, Chris Ure, Richard M. Van Cleave Jr., Jose "Weecho" Velasquez, Samantha Vilfort, Scott Watanabe, Chris Williams, Kelley Williams, Keith Wilson, Emma Wolfe, James Woods, Larry Wu, Zane Yarbrough, and Xinmin Zhao.

Manufactured in Italy.

Design by Jon H. Glick.

COVER Cory Loftis / Digital
CASE Jin Kim / Digital
JACKET FLAPS Cory Loftis / Digital
ENDSHEETS Mehrdad Isvandi / Digital
PAGES 2-3 Scott Watanabe / Digital
THIS PAGE Craig Elliott / Digital
10 9 8 7 6 5 4 3 2 1
Chronicle Books LLC
680 Second Street
San Francisco, California 94107
www.chroniclebooks.com

CONTENTS

PREFACE

ONE OF THE BIGGEST GIFTS that a Walt Disney Animation Studios film can give us is transporting us to places that we would never be able to go to on our own. *Strange World* does exactly that, leading us into a newly discovered realm, full of wondrous creatures and fantastical places unlike anything that has been done in animation. To bring this to life, our artists went above and beyond, inviting us into their imaginations and taking us for the ride of our lives.

This film means a lot to us for many reasons. One of them, of course, is how we have been able to bring characters with different perspectives and backgrounds to life. In past films, such as *Frozen*, *Moana*, and *Encanto*, we have portrayed a beautiful range of female characters and expanded the idea of what a Disney heroine can be. In *Strange World*, we had the opportunity to do the same with our male heroes. [Director] Don Hall, [Co-Director and Writer] Qui Nguyen, and their team of artists worked tirelessly to make sure Searcher, Ethan, and Jaeger were as iconic as they were unique and as relatable as they were dimensional. I've fallen in love with these characters and hope you do too!

At its core, this powerful film deals with the theme of legacy, and every single design decision took that into account. The artists can be proud that they are leaving this film as part of their own legacy to the world, not just because of its aesthetic beauty, but also because of the emotional beauty that they created by breathing life into this story. With that, I welcome you into *Strange World*. Please come on this adventure with us, and discover the process of creating the film through extraordinary art.

—Jennifer Lee, EXECUTIVE PRODUCER AND CHIEF CREATIVE OFFICER, WALT DISNEY ANIMATION STUDIOS

Burny Mattinson / Charcoal

FOREWORD

2017 SEEMS LIKE A LIFETIME AGO. I guess, in a sense, it was. That was the year that *Strange World* came into existence. I had just come off co-directing *Moana* and was ready to start something new. I didn't have to look far for inspiration. It was my kids. That summer, I distinctly remember overhearing a conversation between my two sons, thirteen and ten at the time, and some other kids about climate change. Climate change wasn't real, the other kids claimed. A hoax, they said. My sons countered with logic and facts, and ultimately, the argument ended with neither side convincing the other, and they went back to doing whatever it is kids do at that age, blissfully unaware of the significance of their exchange. It certainly made a profound impression on me, though. I began to think deeply about the world I inherited from my dad, a farmer, and more important, the world my sons will inherit from me. The seed of a story was planted that day: a story about family and adventure, different generations and the world they share; a story about farmers and explorers, undiscovered lands and fantastical creatures; a story about fathers and sons and legacy.

Once planted, this story was nurtured by the intense passion and limitless talent of my fellow storytellers at Disney Animation: fellow farmers and explorers (for what is a storyteller, if not a combination of both?) who bravely followed me into the unknown, while protecting and nourishing the seed of this story until it was ready to grow on its own. This book is a joyful celebration of their compassion, resilience, and astounding artistry.

As the son of a farmer, I grew up hearing the old adage "Care for the land, and the land will care for you." I'd say it applies to stories as well. And this book is evidence that this story has been very, very well cared for. On behalf of my fellow farmers and explorers, we hope it nourishes you as much as it's nourished us.

—Don Hall, DIRECTOR

Don Hall / Digital

9

The Adventure Begins

The first time I walked into the *Strange World* story room was the first time I ever walked into a Disney Animation story room. Going in there and seeing all the sketches blew me away, and I fell in love with the project immediately. Don Hall pitched the film as an *Indiana Jones*–type story but with fathers and sons and a focus on the environment. At that point in my life, I desperately wanted to write films for my kids. *Strange World*, with a message about the environment, was something I could give to them. It was also a super-cool father-and-son love story.
—Qui Nguyen, CO-DIRECTOR AND WRITER

Why Am I Telling This Story?

Philosophical Theme

August 2016
How we, as human beings, live in relationship to the planet is the *fundamental* issue of our time.

Why am I telling this story?

Because of my kids.
When it comes to the environment, I can't honestly say to my kids that the world they're going to inherit will be as good as, let alone better than, the world I inherited.

What can I do?

Recycle, solar panels, drive an electric car . . . it's not enough.
I can tell a story. I can create a film that appeals to all audiences and tells a story that deals with humankind's relationship with the planet.

Philosophically, this is an "Environmental" story

Use entertainment to allow our audience to absorb complex social issues.
        Ex: *Zootopia*

Emotional Theme

"Good Ancestor"

Term designed to make us aware of an expanded sense of time and the enormous generational impacts of our decisions.

Legacy

What do we pass down to future generations?
What do we owe future generations?
What do I owe my sons?
What did I inherit from my father?

I love the idea of telling a story about humankind's relationship with the Earth through the lens of three generations of men, and examining the complications that arise from father/son relationships—the idolization of your father, the criticism of your father, and, ultimately, the acceptance of your father.

So philosophically, this is an "Environmental" story, but thematically and emotionally, it's a story about fathers, sons, and legacy.

ABOVE AND RIGHT Teny Aida Issakhanian / Digital

Craig Elliott / Digital

Every film at Disney Animation begins in a story room, which we completely cover with artwork to remind us about what originally inspired the film. I created this board early on. It inspired my journey into the film and serves as a "true north" for our story, which is the theme of legacy and what we leave behind to our kids. I only needed to glance at this board to remind myself why we were making this film.
—**Don Hall**, DIRECTOR

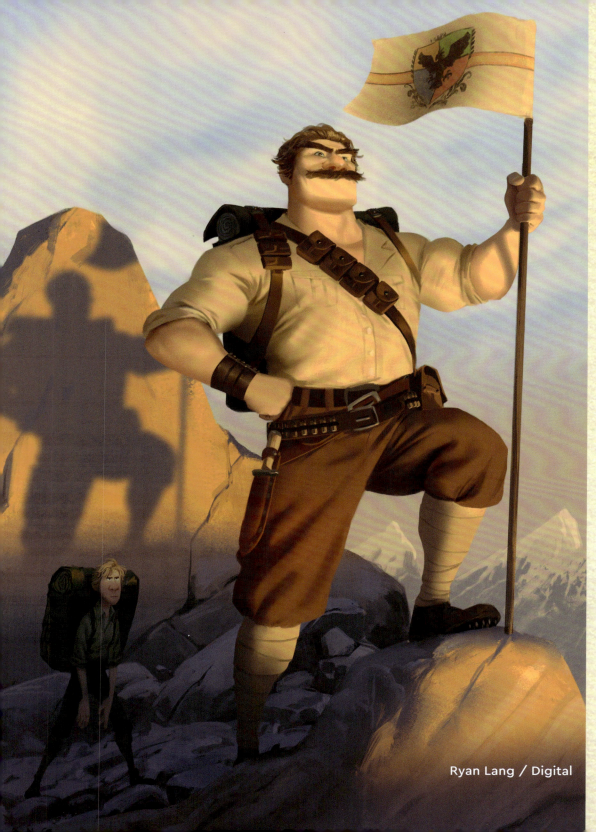

Strange World ends with our characters making a big discovery about their world. To keep the discovery secret, we needed two things: a barrier and the right time period. For the barrier, we surrounded their town with forty-thousand-foot-tall mountains so they couldn't get out. For the time period, we backed into the Industrial Revolution—an era before the existence of modern and digital technology, like satellites, that could make the discovery for them. The Industrial Revolution also happened to be home to many adventure stories about people discovering hidden worlds, valleys, and lands. Those stories led us to a common hero: the archetypal "ultimate man." This hero inspired our first character, Jaeger Clade.

—**Don Hall**, DIRECTOR

Ryan Lang / Digital

Jin Kim / Digital

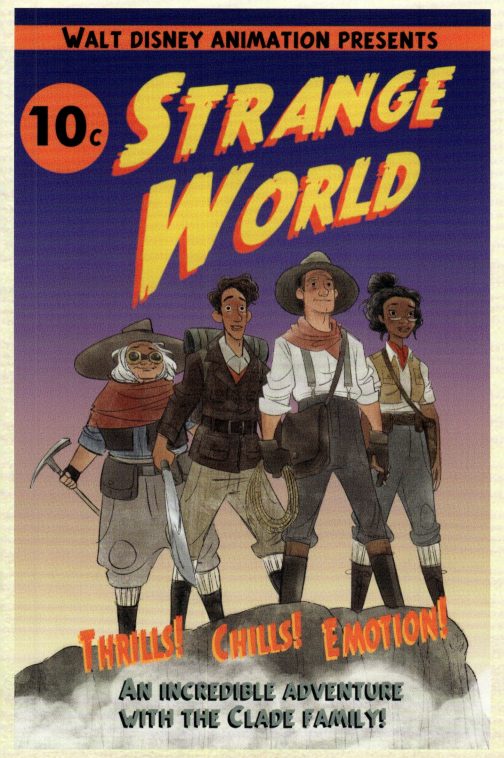

Zane Yarbrough / Digital

One of my first contributions to *Strange World* was saving Jaeger's life. When Don Hall first pitched early story beats to me, he introduced this incredible character, Jaeger Clade, who he had already sketched. I thought Jaeger was so cool. I followed along, waiting for Jaeger's appearance, until we got to a scene in a cave. Then Don said, "This is when Jaeger's son Searcher will find Jaeger's bones." "Wait, what?" I exclaimed. "Yes," Don replied. "Jaeger's bones are going to be in there." I laughed. "So Searcher is going to spend the whole movie searching for his father, only to find out that his father is dead?" Jaeger's been alive ever since.

—Qui Nguyen, CO-DIRECTOR AND WRITER

DOODLES

Don Hall had me hooked at "pulp adventure." I'd been looking forward to partnering with him again since *Big Hero 6*. Knowing his imagination and the incredible worlds he builds, just the title, *Strange World*, excited me. It's an imagined world that is a perfect allegory for our planet.

—Roy Conli, PRODUCER

THIS SPREAD Don Hall / Grease pencil, pen & digital

Joining *Strange World* was the easiest choice for me. Everything started from Don Hall's sketches. From the very beginning, Don, Qui Nguyen, and [Producer] Roy Conli led with vision, clarity, and honesty. I knew we'd make a great team.

—**Mehrdad Isvandi,** PRODUCTION DESIGNER

Jaeger Clade

Jaeger is an older-generation explorer. He's very macho. We designed him big and bulky with huge hands, a large mustache, and body hair everywhere. He carries a big machete that symbolizes his desire to conquer everything in his way. He always has with him all kinds of explorer equipment like ropes, telescopes, canteens, and his compass. His white shirt reflects an explorer look stereotypical of the times. He's the strongest, tallest, and heaviest character in *Strange World*.

—Jin Kim, ART DIRECTOR, CHARACTERS

Jin Kim / Digital

Mehrdad Isvandi & Zachary Angelica Petroc / Digital

Scott Watanabe / Digital

Don Hall / Digital

Even though *Strange World* is a big action-adventure, I didn't want it to lose any comedy. To me that meant moving away from our typical, more realistic house style and toward something different. For our characters, I wanted to find a way to mix inspiration from Hayao Miyazaki films and the pushed style of Franco-Belgian comics. After I pitched the idea to [Production Designer] Mehrdad Isvandi and [Art Director, Characters] Jin Kim to use these as inspiration, Jin returned with rounder, softer characters with oval eyes that felt very unique and warm. We knew we were onto something.

—**Don Hall**, DIRECTOR

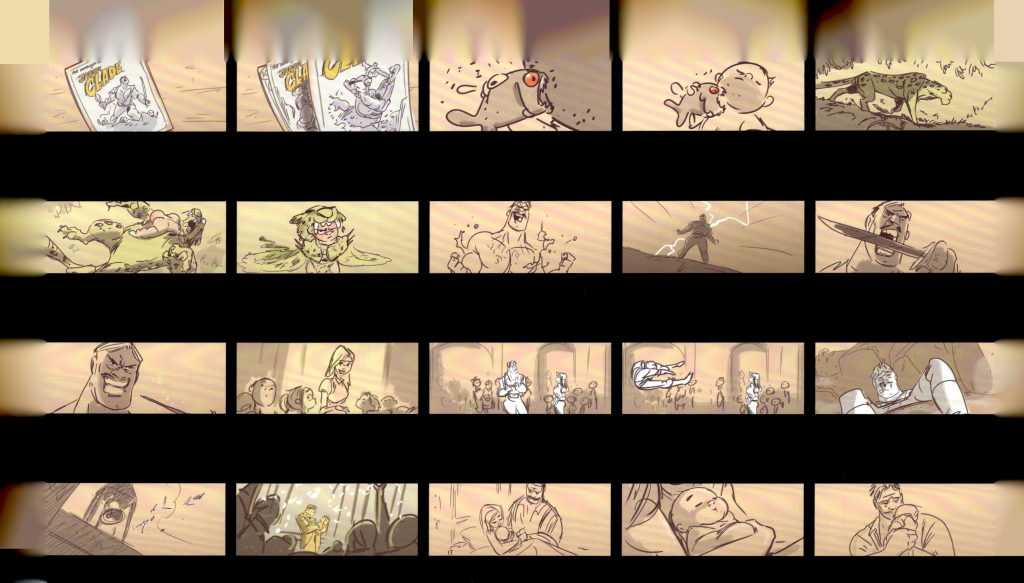

The Ballad of Jaeger Clade

We open the film with a song dedicated to Jaeger Clade. Musical sequences allow us to be less constrained to the realistic settings of our worlds, so I really pushed the boards. I gave Jaeger a mythic, larger-than-life quality and incorporated a bunch of cartoony gags, like him shaving with a piranha. Then I balanced the fun with heartbreaking moments that were true to the story at the time, like Jaeger leaving Searcher, creating a song that

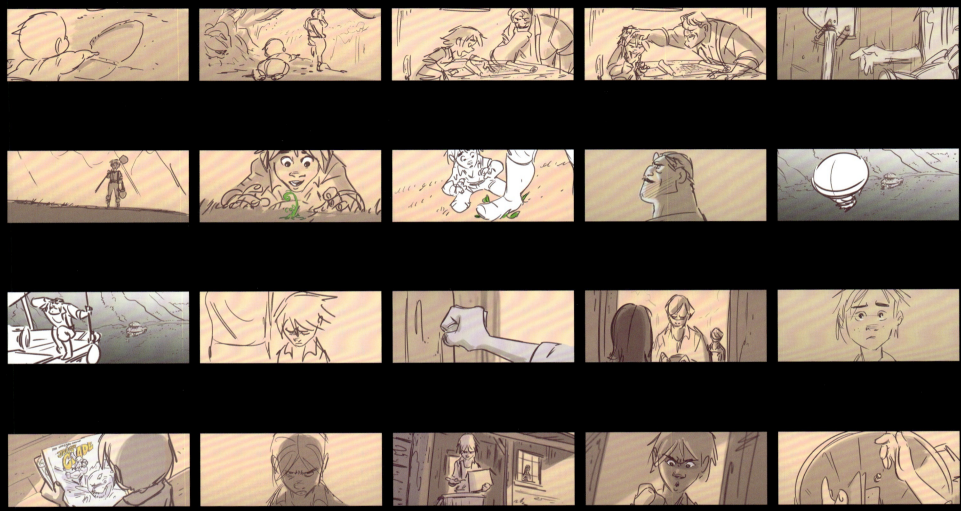

Jeff Snow / Digital

Jin Kim / Digital

MEET THE CLADES

THIS PAGE Don Hall / Digital

SEARCHER CLADE

Searcher came out of a need to find our story's emotional hook. I thought back to the conversations with my sons about the world they were going to inherit, which came from the world I inherited from my dad. Suddenly I knew our story wanted to be intergenerational, about a son, a father, and a grandson. I decided Jaeger's son would be the lead character, not Jaeger, and asked myself, *What if Jaeger's son wanted to be nothing like him?* My dad is a farmer. To me, a farmer is the opposite of an explorer. Farmers are rooted; explorers are not. They're always looking to whatever's beyond the next mountain. Farmers are much more stable. They're about staying where they are and being grounded to the earth.

—**Don Hall**, DIRECTOR

Jin Kim / Digital

Sang Jun Lee / Digital

In the beginning, Searcher was very skinny. When we looked at him against Jaeger, we thought, *How could that small guy come from that big guy?* So we gave Searcher more size and tied father and son together with the same round nose. Searcher's hair was also originally very spiky, but it made him look too young. We played with different hairstyles to age him up and added facial hair.

—**Jin Kim**, ART DIRECTOR, CHARACTERS

Jin Kim / Digital

Jin Kim & SuZan Kim / Digital

25

Jin Kim / Digital

Function and utility were at the forefront of Searcher and Jaeger's costuming. Organic colors allowed their clothing to feel like it was handmade and constructed by their family, without any help from a machine. We also wanted our clothing to feel era-less, like a mix of the past, the present, and the future. Rather than zippers, Searcher's costume utilizes toggles, buttons, and other unique ways of cinching shirts.

—James Woods, VISUAL DEVELOPMENT ARTIST

Various Artists / Digital

ABOVE James Woods / Digital

Jin Kim / Digital

Pando Picker

Sharpened edges

Natural curves

Used and dirty

Larry Wu / Digital

Meg Park / Digital

Sang Jun Lee / Digital

A   B   C

Sang Jun Lee / Digital

Searcher's Pando picker is a sturdy but simple steel spade shovel with a hook. The handle is made from a strong Avalonian tree branch. We kept the tree limb's branching point and slight S curve to give it a natural, unmanufactured look.

—**Larry Wu**, ART DIRECTOR, ENVIRONMENTS

27

Don Hall / Digital

Searcher's Farm

Searcher's farm area uses a lot of horizontals, curves, and hexagons. The farm itself is quaint, charming, and bucolic. We wanted it to be recognizable enough that the audience relates to it but also allow it to have a unique profile.

—**Mehrdad Isvandi**, PRODUCTION DESIGNER

Cory Loftis / Digital

April Liu / Digital

David G. Derrick Jr. / Digital

① POTS

A B C D

② CLOTHESLINE

③ WINDMILL

④ BEEHIVE

Limei Hshieh & Cory Loftis / Digital

Don Hall's early farm designs evoked the cornfields found in his hometown, where the topography tends to be flatter. We knew our fictional world would be surrounded by mountains, so I really wanted Searcher's farm to look like it sat on lands of varying elevation. For inspiration, I looked at hilly farmlands and different types of farms traditionally found in the Alps.

—Scott Watanabe,
VISUAL DEVELOPMENT ARTIST

Cory Loftis / Digital

THIS PAGE April Liu / Digital

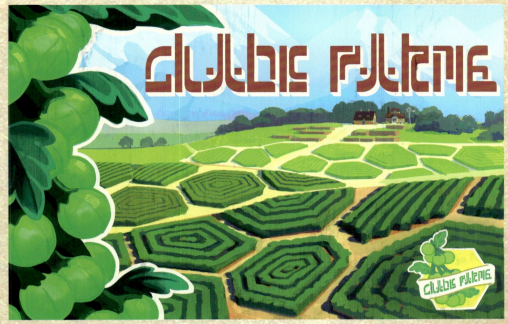

April Liu / Digital

In later designs, we tried to keep the charm and uniqueness from [Visual Development Artist] Scott Watanabe's initial exploration, including the farm layout and the mushroom-roofed style of the Clade family home. Don Hall wanted the home to feel like something Searcher built for his family, so I added lots of small touches like things Searcher might fiddle over when he had a free minute, such as ornamental railings, window frames, and doors. The house has lots of different colored paints on its exterior to suggest that Searcher painted it himself. Circular stained-glass windows also add to the home's personality and charm.

—Cory Loftis, VISUAL DEVELOPMENT ARTIST

Joyce Lee / Digital

Mehrdad Isvandi / Digital

VERY SIMPLE SHUTTERS FOR SMALL FRONT WINDOW.

LOVE THE FEEL OF THESE TIGHTLY THATCHED ROOFS FOR THE FARMHOUSE.

ROUND BRICK CHIMNEY FROM OVEN WITH A METAL RAIN GUARD.

SOME LIGHTLY COLORED DIAMOND GLASS FOR THE KITCHEN.

GINGERBREAD STYLE PORCH WITH MULTICOLOR PAINTWORK ON THE RAILING.

SHINGLES JUST "FLOW" AROUND THE DORMERS AND SMALLER ROOFS.

FEELS MORE LIKE A HOME WITH A SMALL GATE TO THE "FRONT YARD"

Cory Loftis / Digital

33

PANDO

Pando is a miracle plant. It's the oil of this world. The plant produces pods that have an amazing amount of electrical current in them, allowing Avalonians to go from horse and buggy to airships within a very short twenty-five-year time period. All Pando plants are connected underground.

—**Don Hall**, DIRECTOR

Don Hall / Digital

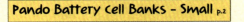

Pando Battery Cell Banks – Small p.2

Single Cell Capsule

Hand Torch

industrial farm Torchlight

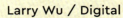

Photographic camera

Larry Wu / Digital

Pando Growth Cycle

April Liu / Digital

THIS PAGE Larry Wu / Digital

The design of Pando was inspired by Brussels sprouts. I made our plant wider and added spirals. Peeling apart the leaves yields the Pando pods, which are fairly simple and round so they could be easily understood. The wild version of Pando is a foot tall with a little bit of pods. The farmed version is three feet tall with large spirals of pods. The Pando pods act like a battery with anodes and cathodes. On top of the Pando plant are long, wispy tassels. Don Hall loved the idea of a visual of a whole field of Pando swaying in the wind like corn.

—**Larry Wu**, ART DIRECTOR, ENVIRONMENTS

Avalonia

Pando Root Growth

BUILDING A FARM . . . AND A FAMILY

This montage showcases the unconditional love Searcher has for his farm, his wife Meridian, and his son Ethan. It has soft moments, funny moments, and, most of all, quiet moments. In real life, when we're with someone we love, we feel a great sense of quiet comfort. Similarly, holding on a shot of Searcher gazing at Ethan can tell us, without using any

THIS SPREAD David G. Derrick Jr., Don Hall, Teny Aida Issakhanian,
Lissa Treiman & Scott Watanabe / Digital

Meridian Clade

A lot of early character exploration for Meridian was spent digging into who she is. Yes, she was a pilot, but that's an occupation, not a personality. *What drew her to flying? Why did she stop flying? What was her life like before Searcher? How did she and Searcher meet? Why did she fall in love with him?* It always felt really natural for her to feel grounded emotionally, even though she was literally up in the air. She's a character who can see the big picture while Searcher tends to hyper-focus, which felt like a good balance in a couple. Design-wise, I always thought it would be cool to give her a look that is a mix of pilot gear and street wear, mixing utility with other feminine elements in a way that helps make her feel like a real, nuanced person.
—Lissa Treiman, HEAD OF STORY

Nicholas Orsi / Digital

Most of our lead characters wear a crossover coat. For Meridian's costume, I mashed up that concept with a flight suit and added exposed wool.

—**Nicholas Orsi**, VISUAL DEVELOPMENT ARTIST

ABOVE AND TOP Jin Kim / Digital

Meridian's plane is an inflatable airship. For its design, we looked for something that wasn't an actual plane but not too far away from one where it might not be recognizable as a plane. The airship has a big inflatable piece on the top that keeps it aloft with dual wings. Meridian used to be a stunt pilot, so her plane can also go really fast. We reflected that in how she sits in the cockpit, as if she's on a motorcycle.

—**Cory Loftis**, VISUAL DEVELOPMENT ARTIST

Cory Loftis / Digital

April Liu / Digital

Mehrdad Isvandi / Digital

Scott Watanabe / Digital

Mehrdad Isvandi & Alessandra Rodriguez Curiel / Digital

Mehrdad Isvandi & Jin Kim / Digital

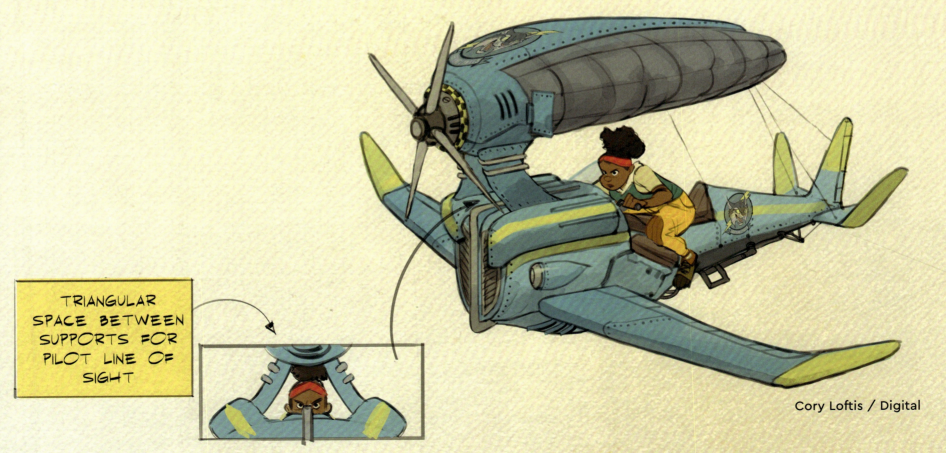

TRIANGULAR SPACE BETWEEN SUPPORTS FOR PILOT LINE OF SIGHT

Cory Loftis / Digital

When Mer was really young she raced the family dog JUST to see how fast she could go. She won sometimes!

Her parents own a bike shop and love teaching her every step to building one.

Meridian is shocked with something she's never seen before - A PLANE.

She falls in love instantly.

Following a scholarship from the Geo Society, Mer graduates with honors for studying aeronautical engineering (very new field)

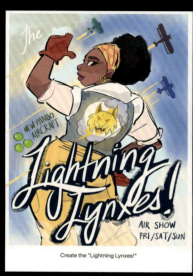
Create the "Lightning Lynxes!"

And saves up to buy her dream hangar! This I where she completes her first plane in order to----

An all femme stunt team that performs regularly for Avalonia

They also throw good parties after awards.

But all this flying needs Pando - good thing theres a small farm nearby that gives them discounts

Meridian and this farmer start spending a lot of time together

LIKE A LOT OF TIME.

She loves pushing him to his absolute comfort limit when they have flying dates.

Searcher confesses his feelings for her

And she returns them

Searcher is also Meridian's number one fan at airshows. He screams the loudest.

When she gets medals she always shoots him a little wave.

Searcher proposes one night with a ring made out of two lug nuts from her hangar. (He gets her a REAL ring later)

But Meridians flights aren't always so smooth

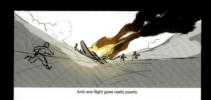
And one flight goes really poorly.

Meridian isnt hurt, but the young couple is definitely shaken.

42

Even more so when Meridian breaks the news that their family is starting!

As much as she loves stunts, Mer has someone that is about to depend on her.

Meridian even builds Ethan his own little toy plane when he's young!

Its 14 years later and Meridian LOVES building model planes / the latest in Avalonia tech. She's still obsessed

And Ethan always sees that Lightning Lynxes jacket around the house.

She sells the stunt plane / buys the crop-duster and Clade Farms is fully realized.

Samantha Vilfort / Digital

A Pilot Is Born

I love that Meridian is a mom. I love that she's a pilot. I love that she has a great relationship with Searcher, and together they love Ethan. I love Meridian so much, I even dreamed up her backstory. Don't let her plane fool you. She used to be a stunt pilot! Not only can Meridian tend the entire Clade family farm, but also she can do it flying her plane in a loop-the-loop, jumping out mid-flight, and timing it just right so it catches her on the way down,
—Samantha Vilfort, STORY ARTIST

Jin Kim / Digital

Don Hall / Digital

Don Hall / Digital

Various Artists / Digital

Don Hall / Digital

ETHAN CLADE

Ethan is a modern teenager. Within our intergenerational story, his experience speaks to the world he and future generations will inherit. We looked at young environmental activists for inspiration. If Jaeger was a conqueror and Searcher was a controller, then it just made sense that Ethan would be a conservationist. Ethan, Searcher, and Jaeger also each represent different perspectives on masculinity: Jaeger the older generation, Ethan the youth, and Searcher the bridge between the two.

—Qui Nguyen, CO-DIRECTOR AND WRITER

Strange World is a utopian place free of prejudice, which isn't the reality of our world. I think it's refreshing and encouraging to see a young character who is freely himself without any idea that he should be anything but who he is. Being LGBTQ+ myself, he is one of the most fulfilling characters I've ever worked on.

—**James Woods,** VISUAL DEVELOPMENT ARTIST

Jin Kim / Digital

Jin Kim / Digital

James Woods / Digital

Jin Kim / Digital

ABOVE AND RIGHT Scott Watanabe / Digital

Ethan has a deep love for his dad, Searcher, although he's conflicted by the internal struggle between who he wants to be and the expectations Searcher puts on him to one day take over the Clade family farm. When Ethan is in the Strange World, he really lights up. In animation, we wanted to sell his awe and fascination with a new world that he'd never before seen.
—Amy Lawson Smeed, HEAD OF ANIMATION

Nicholas Orsi / Digital

Mehrdad Isvandi & Jin Kim / Digital

Scott Watanabe / Digital

April Liu / Digital

THIS PAGE Sang Jun Lee / Digital

LEGEND

Legend is Searcher's dog. He was born with three legs and is very sweet, happy, and loyal. He's a traditional Disney Animation sidekick. For reference, I looked at so many dogs and made so many sketches, including one of a dog that had a muzzle that looked just like Jaeger's mustache. I thought it would be funny for Searcher's dog to constantly remind him of his father, especially in moments where Searcher didn't like Jaeger very much. One of Legend's eyes is always covered by a big fluff of fur.

—**Sang Jun Lee,** VISUAL DEVELOPMENT ARTIST

[Story Artist] Burny Mattinson is the consummate story man. He's been working at Disney Animation since Walt was alive. In a story meeting, he brought up the idea that Searcher should have a dog. His reasoning was sound—we had this exotic character of Splat, but we needed something to help ground us in reality. He was right. Don Hall and Qui Nguyen embraced the idea. Don's nickname for Burny is Legend, so it seemed apropos that we name our dog Legend as a tribute.
—Roy Conli, PRODUCER

ABOVE Scott Watanabe / Digital

Ryan Green / Digital

49

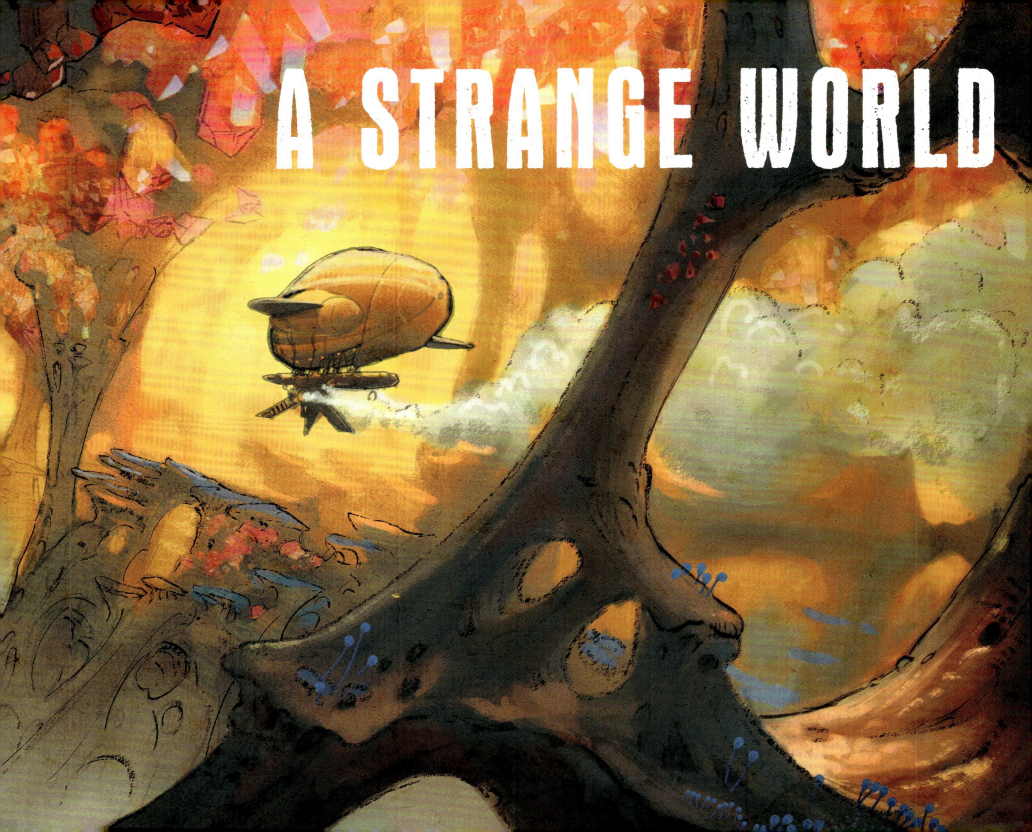

A STRANGE WORLD

STRANGE WORLD EXPLORATION

There is no sun in the Strange World. *So how would we light it?* In this painting, I played with the idea of crystals that could emanate light through light fibers. I wanted the audience to get a feeling of uncertainty, bottomlessness, and scale while sparking their curiosity to want to explore beyond.

In a typical film, we don't have to explain a landscape. A tree is a tree, and a waterfall is a waterfall. A lush, green jungle makes us feel peaceful because our brains know that green equals calm. In the Strange World, a tree might not be a tree; a waterfall might not be a waterfall. Its junglelike landscape is composed of every color except green. As a result, our brains don't know how to feel. We challenged ourselves to design a world that felt otherworldly yet grounded and relatable, and also not too beautiful to be distracting.

—**Mehrdad Isvandi,** PRODUCTION DESIGNER

87

Inside the Strange World

Cory Loftis / Digital

Larry Wu / Digital

Cory Loftis / Digital

Ryan Lang / Digital

Kevin Nelson / Digital

89

The Windy Jungle

Searcher, Ethan, and Meridian enter the Strange World by crashing into the Windy Jungle with their airship, the *Venture*. Early on, we knew the Windy Jungle needed to feel strange, but in our minds, what "strange" meant felt really vague. That was, until we looked at X-rays of the lungs of animals. We studied actual bronchi and bronchial tree systems and added our own version of bronchial trees we named "Pop Trees." Design-wise, they mimic mangroves. Their tops reflect the spherical shape of alveoli air sacs.
—**April Liu**, VISUAL DEVELOPMENT ARTIST

Pop Tree Scale Line-up:

Saplings   Trees   Tree Grouping   Trees Combining   Small Platform   Medium Platform   Huge Platform

Larry Wu / Digital

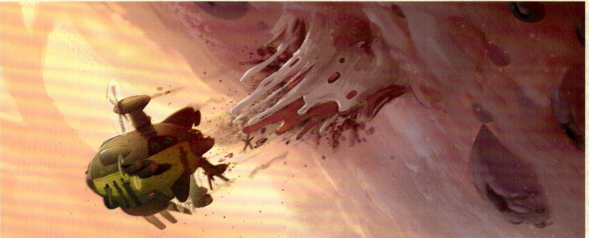

The Bubble Trees

ABOVE AND LEFT Mehrdad Isvandi / Digital

The Windy Jungle is the audience's introduction to the Strange World, so the color needed to be bold and distinct. It is overall magenta and pink in tone. We wanted to have something much more saturated in hue. The Windy Jungle's color also needed to feel unfamiliar and unique. The trick was to have strong, saturated hues and high contrast without it being too visually disorienting. Most important, the goal was to have distinct colors for each region in the Strange World so we never lose track of where we are.

—Justin Cram, ASSOCIATE PRODUCTION DESIGNER

Paul Felix / Digital

THE BURNING SEA

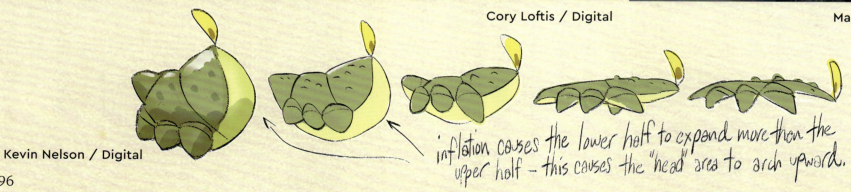

Cory Loftis / Digital

Craig Elliott / Digital

Manu Arenas / Digital

Kevin Nelson / Digital

inflation causes the lower half to expand more than the upper half – this causes the "head" area to arch upward.

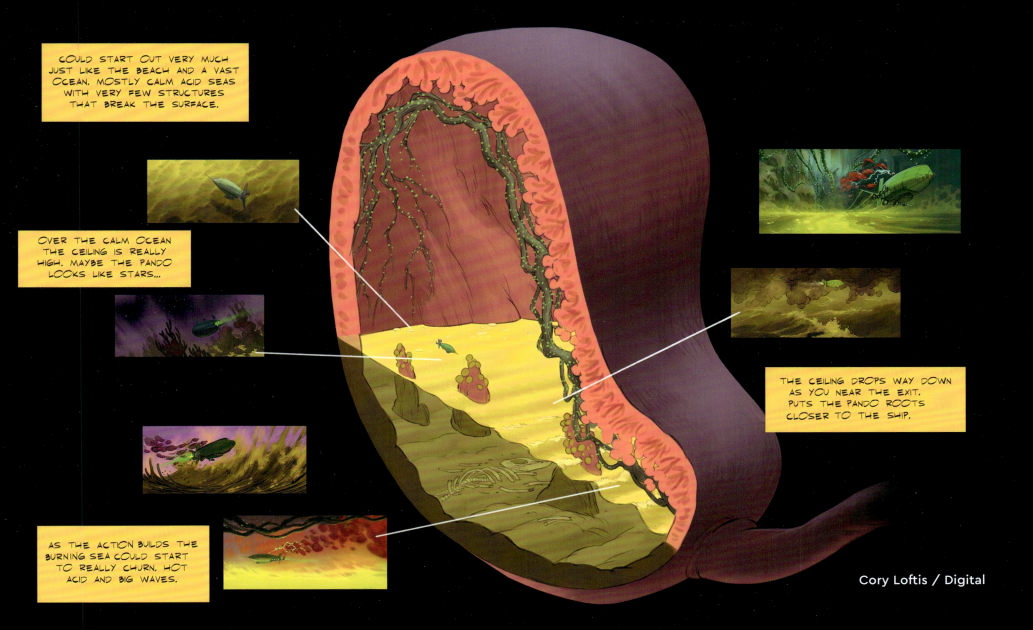

COULD START OUT VERY MUCH JUST LIKE THE BEACH AND A VAST OCEAN. MOSTLY CALM ACID SEAS WITH VERY FEW STRUCTURES THAT BREAK THE SURFACE.

OVER THE CALM OCEAN THE CEILING IS REALLY HIGH. MAYBE THE PANDO LOOKS LIKE STARS...

AS THE ACTION BUILDS THE BURNING SEA COULD START TO REALLY CHURN. HOT ACID AND BIG WAVES.

THE CEILING DROPS WAY DOWN AS YOU NEAR THE EXIT. PUTS THE PANDO ROOTS CLOSER TO THE SHIP.

Cory Loftis / Digital

The Burning Sea is supposed to be a *mood* and a *feeling*. Technically it's a giant acid lake full of sulfur and other kinds of gasses. The atmosphere has a thick feel to it, inspired by some old fantasy paintings I found, and the liquid in the Burning Sea is thick and viscous, reminiscent of a mix of acid and food. I added a lot of bubble shapes, fun shapes, and nasty things that could explode or pop, inspired by stomach ulcers. Essentially, the Burning Sea is one big, treacherous whoopee cushion.

—Cory Loftis, VISUAL DEVELOPMENT ARTIST

Larry Wu / Digital

Luna Glade

Walking through a glade of these trees would be a really magical experience. As a character steps near an individual tree, it lights up. Each tree is modeled after an individual nerve cell. Similar to what nerves do in the body, the lights are our version of electrical pulses, which we imagined would be blue in color. We made Luna Glade large and expansive but dark to give the audience a visual break from other more colorful areas in the Strange World. The canopy and roots also mimic the dendritic fingers of a nerve cell and the trunks mimic the axons.

—**Larry Wu**, ART DIRECTOR, ENVIRONMENTS

arms lengthen when needed

When the arms are in, the animal can spin in the air

Kevin Nelson / Digital

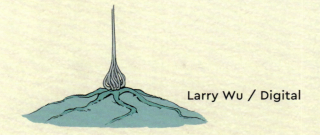

Larry Wu / Digital

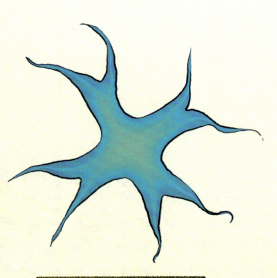

Dendrite Top View

4 pairs of dendritic tendrils.

When active, particulates are released.

Double Dendrite Layer

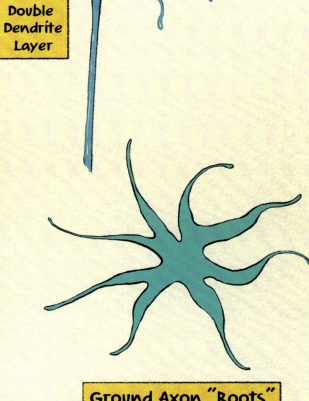

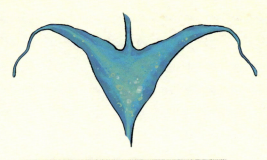

Dendrite Cross Section

They never become paper thin. There should appear to be a more solid center, that glows brighter when active.

The axon trunks have subtle bends and slight non-uniform thickness.

Soft and smooth exterior skin. Solid jelly-like interior with particulates.

Ground Axon "Roots"

The Luna Glade ground is mostly barren with just a couple other organisms sprinkled about. It is also uneven, defined by the mounds under each tree.

Axon Terminals

There are 8 lateral and 4 medial tendrils. The terminals have a rougher texture.

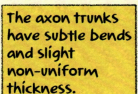

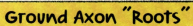

Larry Wu / Digital

Larry Wu / Digital

April Liu / Digital

Paul Felix / Digital

The Amber Desert

The Amber Desert is part of a montage of shots, so, like the Burning Sea, it's more of a backdrop environment. The entrance has a waterfall where large, floating, particulate, liquid bubbles splatter on the *Venture* as it moves through them, mimicking rain. The inside of the Amber Desert is inspired by desert landscapes and microphotographs of pancreases, which included bluish, round parts. We imagined those bluish, round parts could be giant cloud creatures that would congregate in what appeared to be pools of blue stuff that lift up as the *Venture* flies through and disturbs their environment.

—**Mehrdad Isvandi, PRODUCTION DESIGNER**

April Liu / Digital

Paul Felix / Digital

Ryan Lang / Digital

Limei Hshieh / Digital

Limei Hshieh / Digital

The Mirrored Mesas

The Mirrored Mesas are a canyon-like environment, but unlike the Grand Canyon, the canyons here are below *and* above. I was really inspired by [Visual Development Artist] Kevin Nelson and [Visual Development Artist] Nicholas Orsi's designs to create shapes that resemble "islands" that could also move like creatures. The Mirrored Mesas are part of a montage and intended to be a very beautiful scene, so we channeled organic and figurative qualities of semi-abstract monumental bronze sculptures.

—**Limei Hshieh,** VISUAL DEVELOPMENT ARTIST

THIS PAGE **Limei Hshieh** / Digital

105

Paul Felix / Digital

Larry Wu / Digital

The Petrified Cave

My early exploration of the Petrified Cave had a very pulpy feel. The film climaxes there, so I added a ton of energy and weather, like lightning bolts of Pando electricity crackling through the sky. We imagined the Petrified Cave was a rock sculpture that would beat, like a heart. For inspiration, I looked at basalt column formations and imagined them pulsing and rippling out. To show life returning to the Petrified Cave, I pitched the idea that it would grow giant, wavy betta fish-like, or jellyfish-like, fins. I loved the idea of our characters being rewarded with a spectacular show of life blooming before their eyes.

—**Scott Watanabe**, VISUAL DEVELOPMENT ARTIST

THIS PAGE Paul Felix / Digital

Larry Wu / Digital

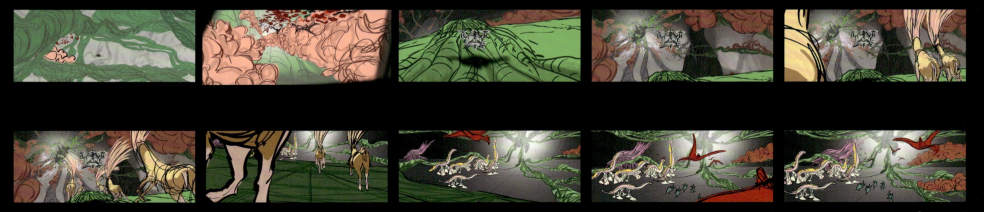

Julia "Fitzy" Fitzmaurice / Digital

Paul Felix / Digital

Paul Felix / Digital

Scott Watanabe / Digital

Scott Watanabe / Digital

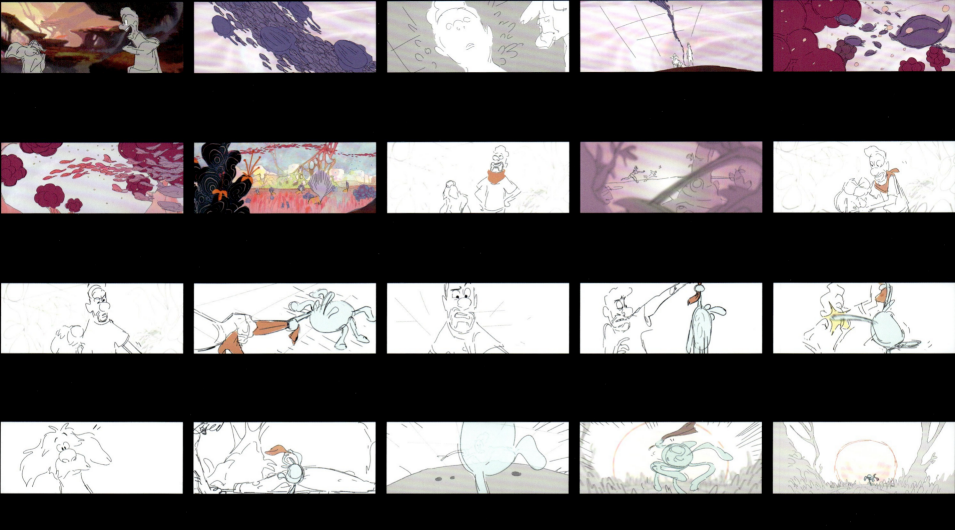

DISCOVERING STRANGE WORLD

In this sequence, I had to juggle three key beats: an introduction to the Strange World; a fake introduction to the character Splat; and a reintroduction to Jaeger, who was trapped in the Strange World for years. I shot the scene to put the audience in Searcher's point of view, as he looks at what at first appears to be a monstrous creature that is revealed, shockingly, to be Jaeger, his long-lost father. Visually, I also thought it would be fun to give Jaeger a flamethrower he made himself as a weapon.
—Javier Ledesma Barbolla, STORY ARTIST

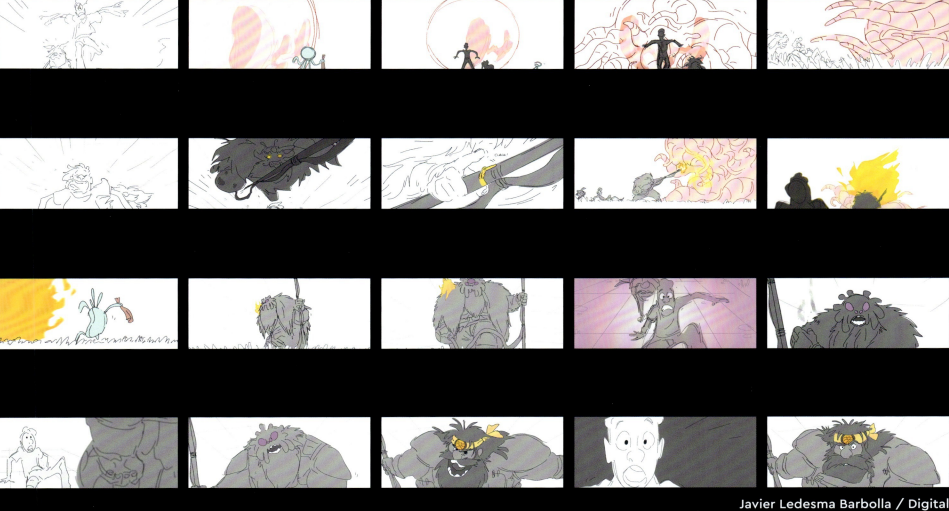

Don Hall / Digital

SPLAT

Chris Ure / Digital

Don Hall / Digital

Splat lives in the Strange World. Its design is based on an immune system cell, known as a dendritic cell, which are the scouts of the immune system. They're kind of like little thieves, sussing out new things that enter the body and stealing parts of it to present to the attack cells.

—**Don Hall**, DIRECTOR

Chris Williams / Digital

Mike Gabriel / Digital

Don Hall / Digital

Don Hall / Digital

Splat was the very first character we designed. We wanted to make Splat as appealing as possible, very likeable and huggable, like the character Baymax from *Big Hero 6*, but even more simple than Baymax, who has eyes but not a mouth. Splat has no eyes and no mouth! It has only legs and arms. Its initial design was a big bowl shape with long legs. When Splat first came to life in initial walk and run tests, everyone fell in love with the character.
—Jin Kim, ART DIRECTOR, CHARACTERS

115

In the beginning, Splat's designs looked like they were based off jellyfish and octopi, sometimes having faces, sometimes not. Don Hall then pitched looking at pantomime for inspiration, removing the eyes and mouth entirely. Having a character, similar to *Aladdin*'s Magic Carpet, that would have to communicate completely visually was inspiring and energizing to all the artists on the film. And Splat as we know it was born.
—**Mehrdad Isvandi, PRODUCTION DESIGNER**

THIS PAGE Jin Kim / Digital

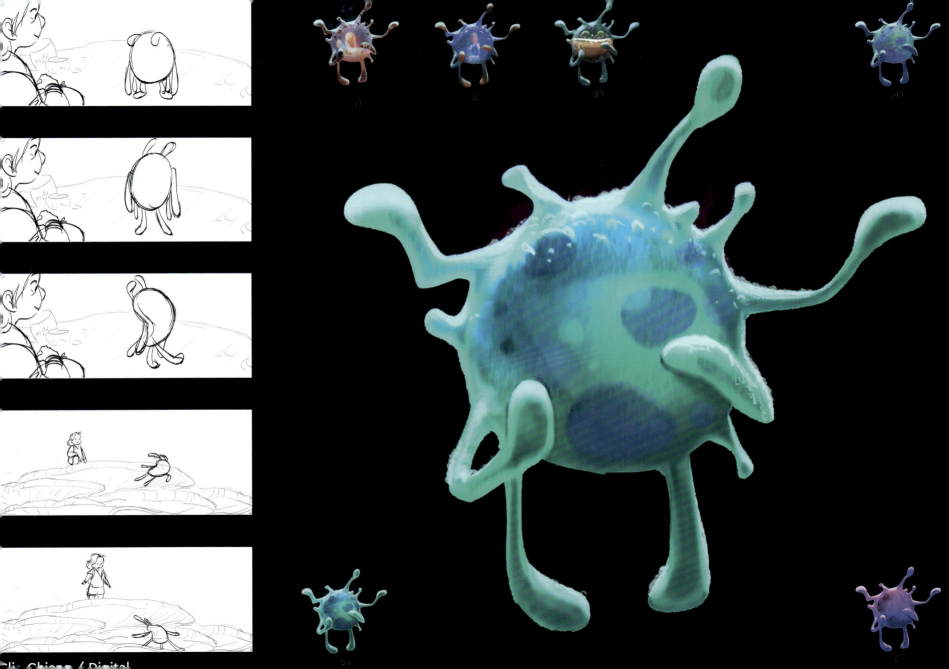

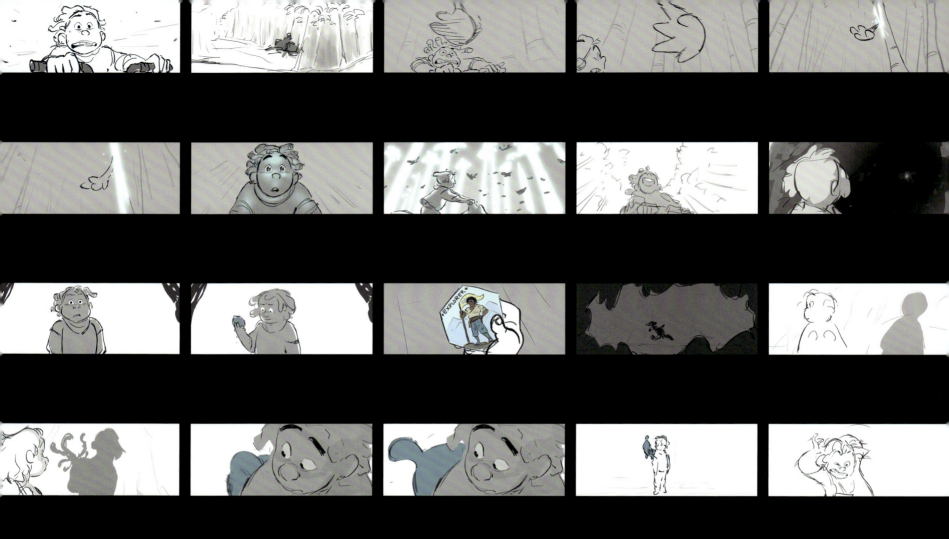

MEET SPLAT

Ethan begins this sequence falling in love with the sights and sounds of the Strange World, when suddenly, like a horror film, a terrifying shadow appears behind him. It's Splat! Ethan and Splat begin to connect. Boarding this sequence, I tried to get as much entertainment as possible while also playing with the audience's expectations

Doyenne Callisto Mal

Doyenne Callisto Mal bravely leads the expedition into the Strange World. She is a strong and experienced explorer and a deeply empathetic and capable leader, driven by a desire to do what is best for the Avalonian people. In earlier versions of the story, Callisto was Jaeger's rough-and-tumble protégé who wanted nothing more than to be the next great explorer. She's a thrilling character with good intentions who has to challenge her own perspectives to make the right decision.

—Laurie Au, ASSOCIATE PRODUCER

Sang Jun Lee / Digital

Various Artists / Digital

Various Artists / Digital

Sang Jun Lee / Digital

Scott Watanabe / Digital

Jin Kim / Digital

James Woods / Digital

Sang Jun Lee / Digital

Jin Kim / Digital

121

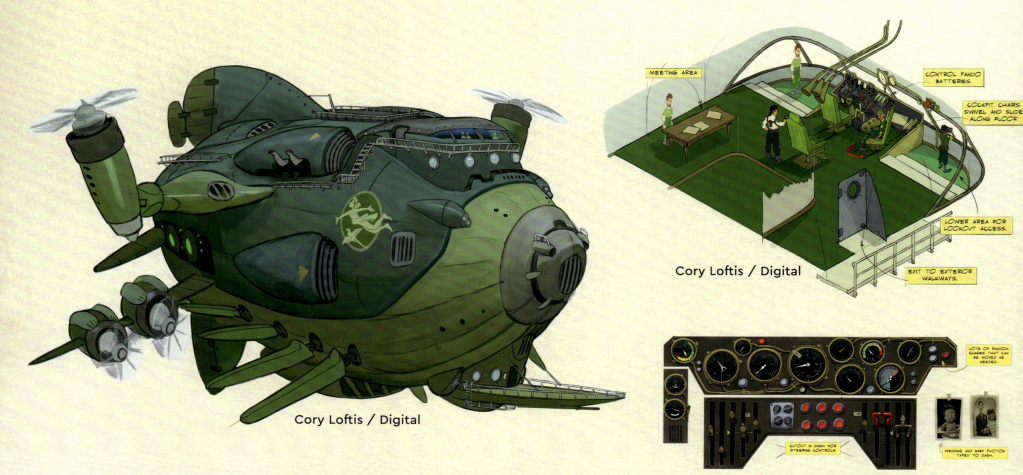

MEETING AREA

CONTROL PANDO BATTERIES

COCKPIT CHAIRS SWIVEL AND SLIDE ALONG FLOOR

LOWER AREA FOR LOOKOUT ACCESS.

EXIT TO EXTERIOR WALKWAYS.

Cory Loftis / Digital

LOTS OF RANDOM GUAGES THAT CAN BE MOVED AS NEEDED.

CUTOUT IN DASH FOR STEERING CONTROLS

WEDDING AND BABY PHOTOS TAPED TO DASH.

Cory Loftis / Digital

Cory Loftis / Digital

Scott Watanabe / Digital

122

The Venture

The *Venture* was pitched to me as the ultimate expression of Avalonian exploration. For its design, I referenced real aircraft, including bombers, spacecraft, and airships like zeppelins and blimps. Don Hall really wanted the *Venture* to move at speed. But most airships are like hot air balloons, which only go up. You can't really control where they land. Therefore, I added a real engine, control sets, wings, a believable cockpit, and propellers along the top that allow for roll.

—**Cory Loftis,** VISUAL DEVELOPMENT ARTIST

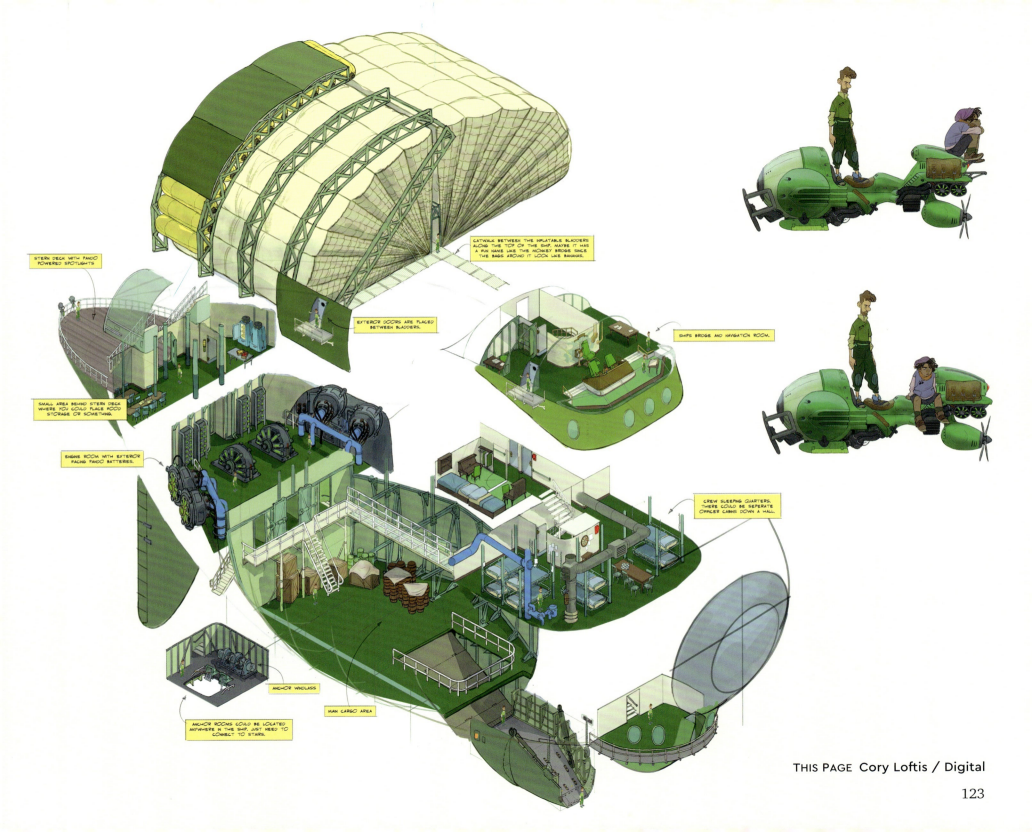

STERN DECK WITH PANDO POWERED SPOTLIGHTS

CATWALK BETWEEN THE INFLATABLE BLADDERS ALONG THE TOP OF THE SHIP. MAYBE IT HAS A FUN NAME LIKE THE MONKEY BRIDGE SINCE THE BAGS AROUND IT LOOK LIKE BANANAS.

EXTERIOR DOORS ARE PLACED BETWEEN BLADDERS.

SHIPS BRIDGE AND NAVIGATION ROOM.

SMALL AREA BEHIND STERN DECK WHERE YOU COULD PLACE FOOD STORAGE OR SOMETHING.

ENGINE ROOM WITH EXTERIOR FACING PANDO BATTERIES.

CREW SLEEPING QUARTERS. THERE COULD BE SEPERATE OFFICER CABINS DOWN A HALL.

ANCHOR ROOMS COULD BE LOCATED ANYWHERE IN THE SHIP, JUST NEED TO CONNECT TO STAIRS.

ANCHOR WINDLASS

MAIN CARGO AREA

THIS PAGE Cory Loftis / Digital

123

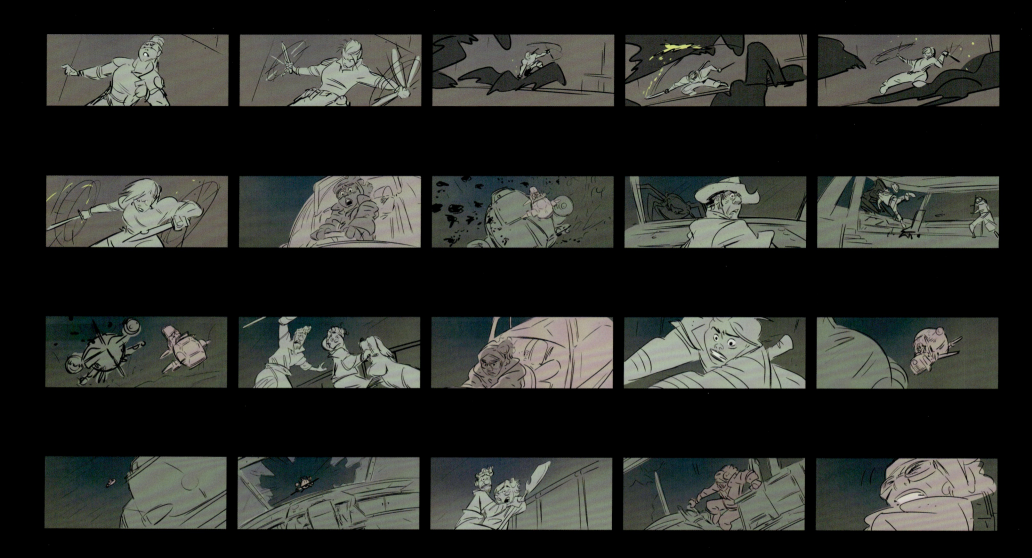

ᛏᴇʀʀᴏʀ ɪɴ ᴛʜᴇ Sᴋɪᴇꜱ

In these boards, Meridian saves the *Venture* from crash-landing into the Strange World. I wanted to establish her as an action hero, like a James Bond, so I really pushed the tension. I worked on a few iterations, including one where she rockets in on her plane, leaps onto the *Venture* as it hurtles toward the ground, and regains control of the out-of-control airship.

—Jeff Snow, STORY ARTIST

David G. Derrick Jr. / Digital

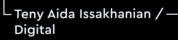

Teny Aida Issakhanian /
Digital

Jeff Snow / Digital

125

The Venture Crew

When thinking about the characters who would make up the crew of the *Venture*, we wanted to reflect the dimensions of Avalonia. Within the team consisting of an engineer, a chef, a medic, a shipmate officer, an air traffic controller, a pilot, and more, we have people representing different racial backgrounds, body types, and gender identities, including non-binary characters like Captain Pulk.
—**Qui Nguyen**, CO-DIRECTOR AND WRITER

Scott Watanabe / Digital

Sang Jun Lee / Digital

126

Jin Kim / Digital

Kevin Nelson / Digital

Berth   Fathom   Reef   Caspian   Cape   Narissa   Duffle   Ervina   Hardy

Sang Jun Lee / Digital

127

Meet The Crew

My first stab at design for the *Venture* crew included some really wild characters. I designed a knife thrower, a mystic, a game warden, and even a giant so that, compared to them, Searcher would really stick out.

—**Chris Ure,** STORY ARTIST

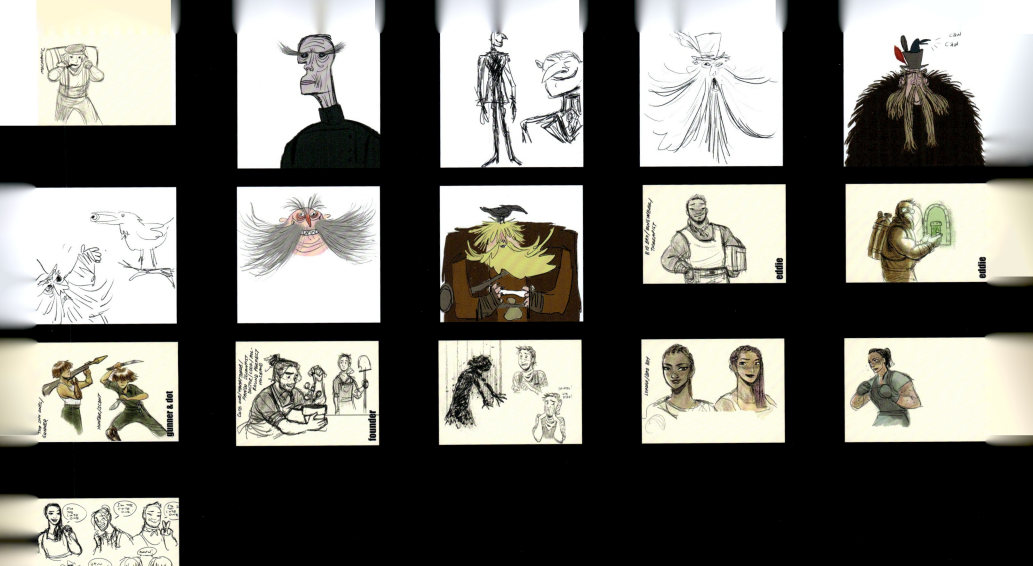

THIS SPREAD Chris Ure & Clio Chiang / Mixed mediums

Later on, we reimagined the characters. I thought of them as a K-pop band and designed each to be an archetype, like the leader, the cute one, and the standoffish one. One was even a better-looking version of Searcher. I also got to decide who was expendable and would be taken out by Strange World monsters. The Searcher doppelgänger made the expendable list.

Chris Ure / Digital

Mehrdad Isvandi & Jin Kim / Digital

Chris Ure / Digital

Chris Ure / Digital

Wears exoskeleton parts as camoflauge to sneak past hostile creatures

A NEW JAEGER

Jaeger survived in the Strange World for some twenty-five years. I don't know how he did, but of course he did. In the real world, when a person is isolated and kept in one area by themselves, they can go a little crazy. Somehow, Jaeger stayed sane. He's still the same Jaeger. Instead of a machete, he made a flamethrower. His shoulder pads and armor are made from the dead skin of Strange World creatures he found along the way, sewn together to wear as protection.

—Jin Kim, ART DIRECTOR, CHARACTERS

Jin Kim / Digital

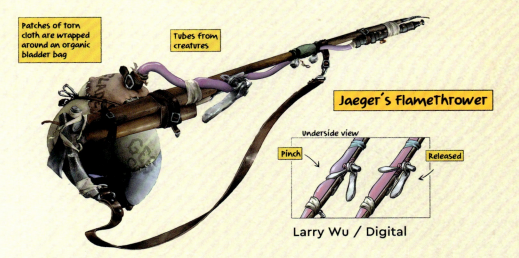

Patches of torn cloth are wrapped around an organic bladder bag

Tubes from creatures

Jaeger's Flamethrower

Underside view

Pinch

Released

Larry Wu / Digital

Jaeger's flamethrower mimics an old-timey musket and is fashioned from the mountaineering, hiking, and climbing tools he brought on his initial expedition mixed with materials he found in the Strange World. The gas is held in a bag he created using organic material from the Strange World. Wrapped around the bag is a protective layer of fabric he patched together from his backpack and blanket. A purple tube formed from the remnants of Strange World creatures to transport the gas from the bag to the front of the flamethrower adds a fun pop of color.
—**Larry Wu**, ART DIRECTOR, ENVIRONMENTS

Jin Kim / Digital

Jin Kim / Digital

Scott Watanabe / Digital

Ryan Lang / Digital

Don Hall / Digital

Samantha Vilfort / Digital

Meg Park / Digital

THREE MEN

When we tell stories, we draw from our own lives. I'm named after my father, and I immediately connected with the pressure of the father-son dynamic. I identified with Searcher and his desire to be different from his legendary father, Jaeger Clade. Ironically, when Searcher imposes his "legacy" on Ethan, he finds himself repeating the same mistakes his father made. As hard as we try as parents, we still make mistakes—sometimes the same ones our parents made.
—David G. Derrick Jr., HEAD OF STORY

JAEGER   SEARCHER   ETHAN

Jin Kim / Digital

Don Hall / Digital

Larry Wu / Digital

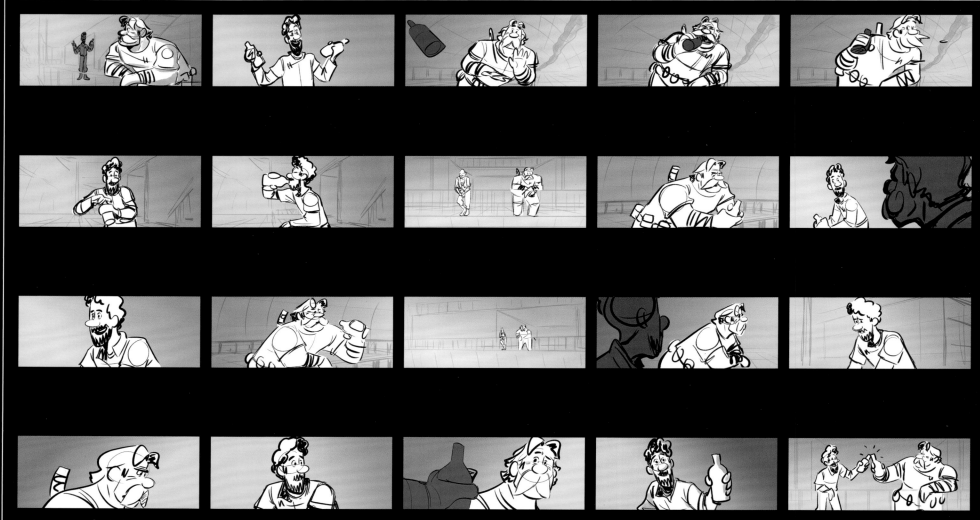

Tyre Jones / Digital

FAMILY IS FOREVER

My primary focus in this sequence was to show the complex emotional experience of a father and son who desperately want a relationship but who don't know how to relate, all while keeping the pacing of the scene. Here, over a meal and for the first time ever, Jaeger and Searcher finally connect. I really wanted the audience to feel hope that these two characters who love each other might actually forgive one another someday.

—Tyre Jones, STORY ARTIST

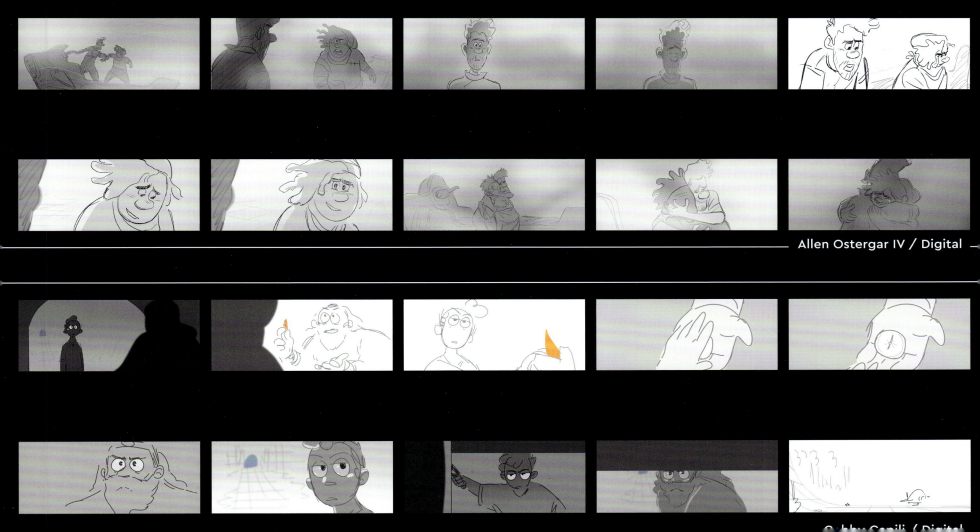

Paul Felix / Digital

Craig Elliott / Digital

Kevin Nelson / Digital

James Woods / Digital

Monsters and Creatures

Our creatures in the Strange World find the unexpected through surprising actions, changes in shape, unusual colors, and presence in unpredictable locations. Many have an under-the-sea feel. I looked at the cooperative behaviors of some marine organisms, like fish that school, the filter-feeding qualities of colonies of coral and barnacles next to terrestrial organisms, and cells and other organic material we looked at under a microscope. From that exploration came many creatures, including the Filterlopes that herd like antelopes but have filtering appendages that help them passively clean an environment.
—**Kevin Nelson,** VISUAL DEVELOPMENT ARTIST

the "beak" allows us to see the "head" turn

Kevin Nelson / Digital

Filterlope

straight lines run thru the back of neck to the front leg

¾

also front of leg to the rear

even when filter is retracted, it still protrudes as the head/antlers

We took a big creative swing with the Goblinswills. They are reminiscent of dolphins and are not defined or inhibited by any kind of outward structure. They are almost like a flock of birds or a school of fish that swoop in elegantly to feed off the Pop Trees.

—**Don Hall,** DIRECTOR

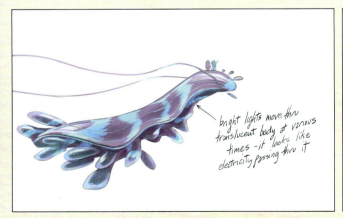

bright lights move thru translucent body at various times - it looks like electricity passing thru it

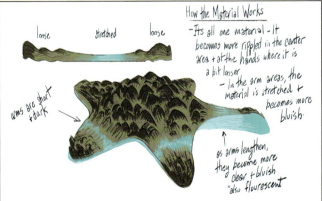

How the Material Works

- Its all one material - It becomes more rippled in the center area + at the hands where it is a bit looser
- In the arm areas, the material is stretched + becomes more bluish.

loose   stretched   loose

arms are short + dark

as arms lengthen, they become more clear + bluish "also flourescent

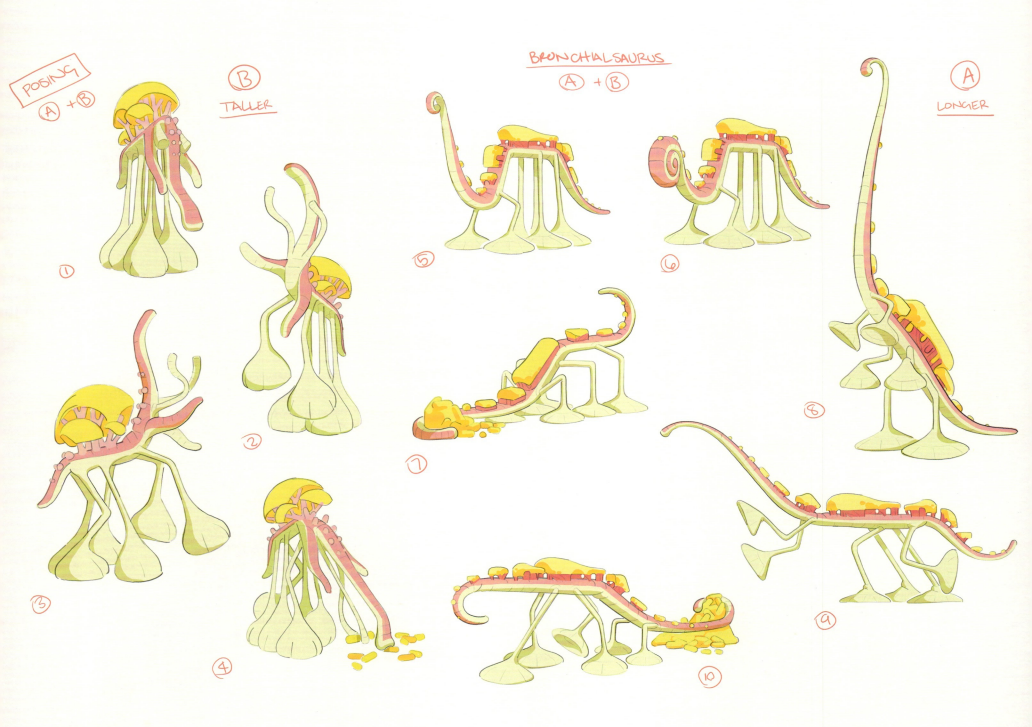

BRONCHIALSAURUS

POSING Ⓐ +Ⓑ

Ⓑ TALLER

Ⓐ +Ⓑ

Ⓐ LONGER

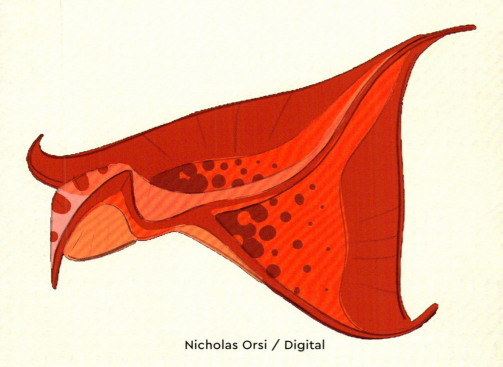

Nicholas Orsi / Digital

When designing the Strange World creatures, I tried to distill each one down to its singular purpose or task. For example, the Transportasaurses are essentially giant ropes. Their whole purpose is to collect, gather, and throw things. In one version, I designed them to be flat to the ground, rolling up on debris collected on the surface. In another, I gave them long, ropy appendages that could wrap around bacteria and other foreign objects.

—**Nicholas Orsi,** VISUAL DEVELOPMENT ARTIST

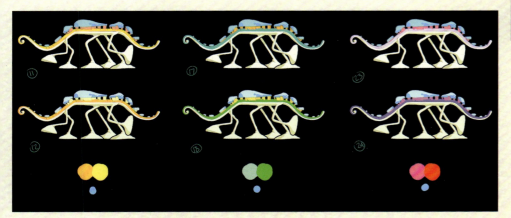

Nicholas Orsi / Digital

Mehrdad Isvandi & James Woods / Digital

April Liu / Digital

Kevin Nelson / Digital

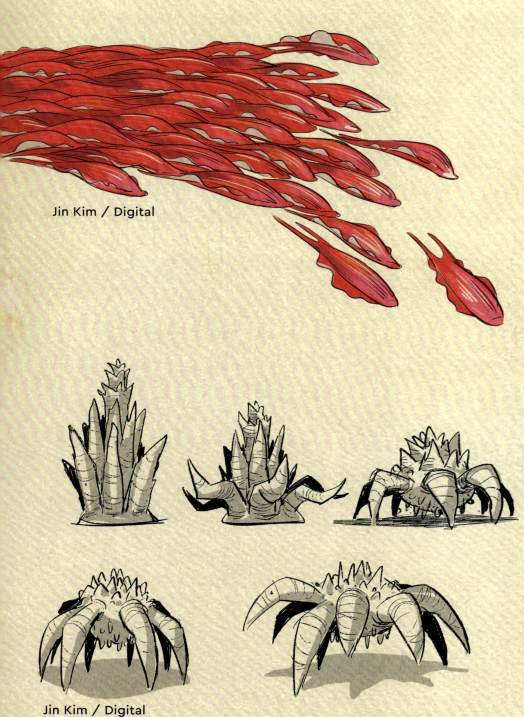

Jin Kim / Digital

Jin Kim / Digital

I love how everything in *Strange World* is so imaginative. Our characters are being stretched and pushed in ways that are reminiscent of classic Disney characters, like Ichabod Crane from *The Legend of Sleepy Hollow* and Roger from *One Hundred and One Dalmatians*. Though we're in CG, our characters have a hand-drawn charisma to them. We've even had to create our own glossary of terms to talk about creatures, their environments, and what sounds they're all making. It's ridiculous what we've had to make up just to talk about the film as collaborators.

—**Qui Nguyen,** CO-DIRECTOR AND WRITER

James Woods / Digital

The cloud o'war is playfully familiar at first sight with photorealistic cloud qualities, yet it becomes more mysterious upon closer observation. Bands of pastel illumination run through its dense internal structure, which behaves like both a vapor and solid material.
—**Michael Kaschalk**, HEAD OF EFFECTS

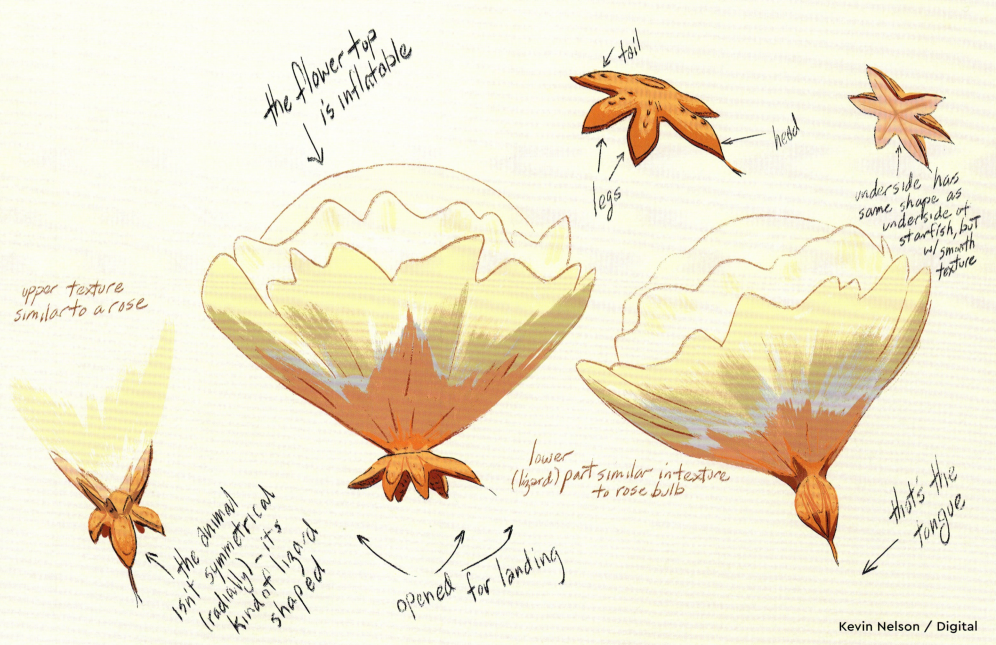

the flower top is inflatable

upper texture similar to a rose

↖ tail

head

legs

underside has same shape as underside of starfish, but w/ smooth texture

the animal isn't symmetrical (radially) — it's kind of lizard shaped

lower (lizard) part similar in texture to rose bulb

opened for landing

that's the tongue

Kevin Nelson / Digital

Ryan Lang / Digital

ABOVE Kevin Nelson / Digital

148

Kevin Nelson / Digital

Kevin Nelson / Digital

Kevin Nelson / Digital

Don Hall / Digital

149

Chaos!

Lower Extremities Are Doing All The Work

Gruesome Lift

Eric Hutchison / Digital

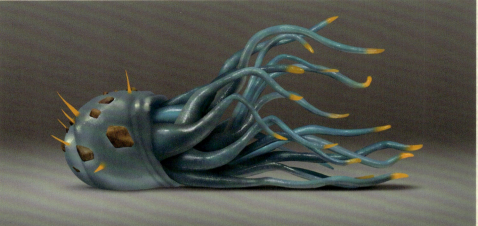

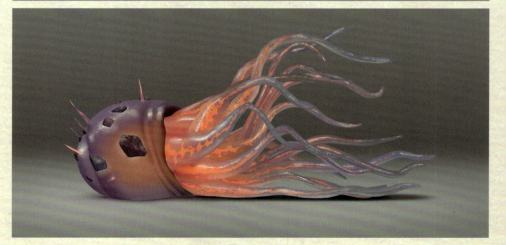

REAPERS

The Reapers are inspired by macrophages, or white blood cells, that send out tentacle-like appendages to grab bacteria and foreign objects to clear them out of the body. To up the creepy factor, I added inspiration from microbial life in rivers, including cells that looked like spiders that could invert themselves, and mixed in my own reference, like translucent eggs with aliens squirming around inside. For fun I experimented with how they might act when threatened or what they might look like with long appendages reminiscent of daddy longlegs spiders.

—**Nicholas Orsi,** VISUAL DEVELOPMENT ARTIST

Ryan Lang & Alena Loftis / Digital

PAGE ③

FULL-COURT PRESS!!!

① FINGERS

② FINGERS REACH OUT FROM BODY.

③ FRANETIC TAPE WORM FINGERS

④ TENTACLES FORTIFY EXPOSURE + BREAK OFF INTO FINGERS

⑤ FINGERS GROW + SPROUT MORE

⑥ FINGERS BLOAT + MULTIPLY IN ALGORITHMIC FRACTAL GROWTH.

⑦ SEA CUCUMBER-ISH + FRACTAL GROWTH

⑧ FORTIFIES MUSCLES + TENDONS + NERVES + ARTERIES + VEINS

THIS PAGE Nicholas Orsi / Digital

A NEW WORLD

Scott Watanabe / Digital

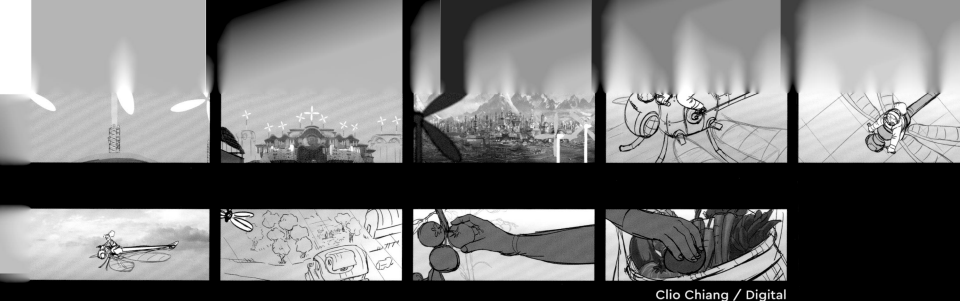

Clio Chiang / Digital

A Better Tomorrow

Every Disney Animation film pushes our capacity for storytelling to new levels, and *Strange World* is no exception. Together as a crew, we've achieved a number of groundbreaking firsts, like tasking our character animators to animate an environment that is totally alive, both literally and figuratively, and bringing to screen the representation of characters and character interactions in ways never before seen. Working on this film has brought me a tremendous amount of pride.
—Steve Goldberg, VISUAL EFFECTS SUPERVISOR

Ryan Lang / Digital

Ryan Lang / Digital

David G. Derrick Jr. / Digital

At its heart, this is a story about legacy. What we leave for future generations can either be a burden or gift. As we discover through the story of the Clades, legacy isn't about leaving statues behind. Legacy is leaving the world a better, healthier place for future generations.

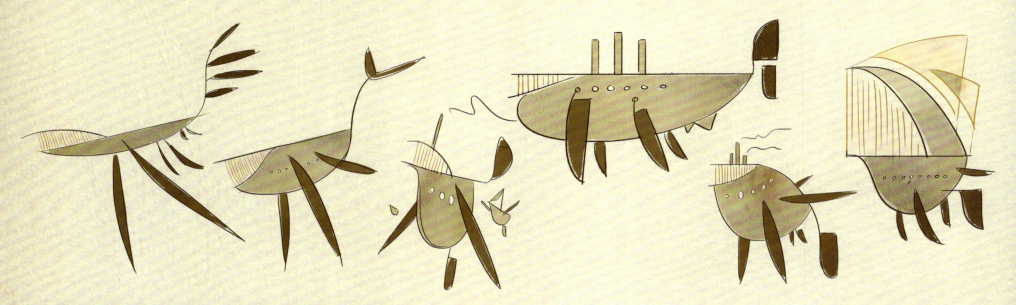

What does a better tomorrow, environmentally speaking, look like in Avalonia? To answer that question, we explored many ideas, including looking into urban agriculture and eco-friendly farming practices. Then, we started imagining that the entire city might turn into one giant sustainable farm. In the air, I imagined these robotic whale-like airships that could filter carbon dioxide and pollution, similarly to how whales strain plankton from the ocean.

—Camille Andre, VISUAL DEVELOPMENT ARTIST

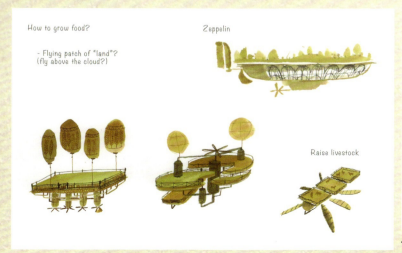

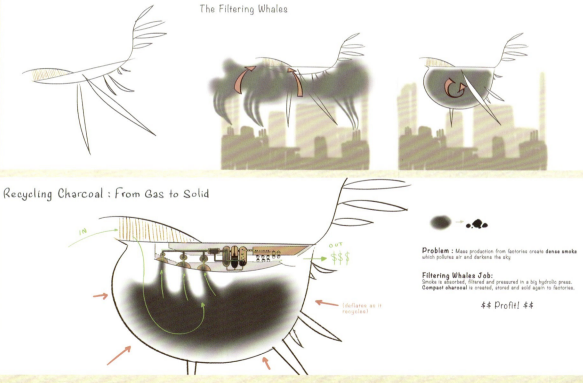

The Filtering Whales

Recycling Charcoal : From Gas to Solid

IN

OUT $$$

Problem : Mass production from factories create **dense smoke** which pollutes air and darkens the sky

Filtering Whales Job:
Smoke is absorbed, filtered and pressured in a big hydrolic press. **Compact charcoal** is created, stored and sold again to factories.

(deflates as it recycles)

$$ Profit! $$

How to grow food?

- Flying patch of "land"? (fly above the cloud?)

Zeppelin

Raise livestock

THIS SPREAD Camille Andre / Digital

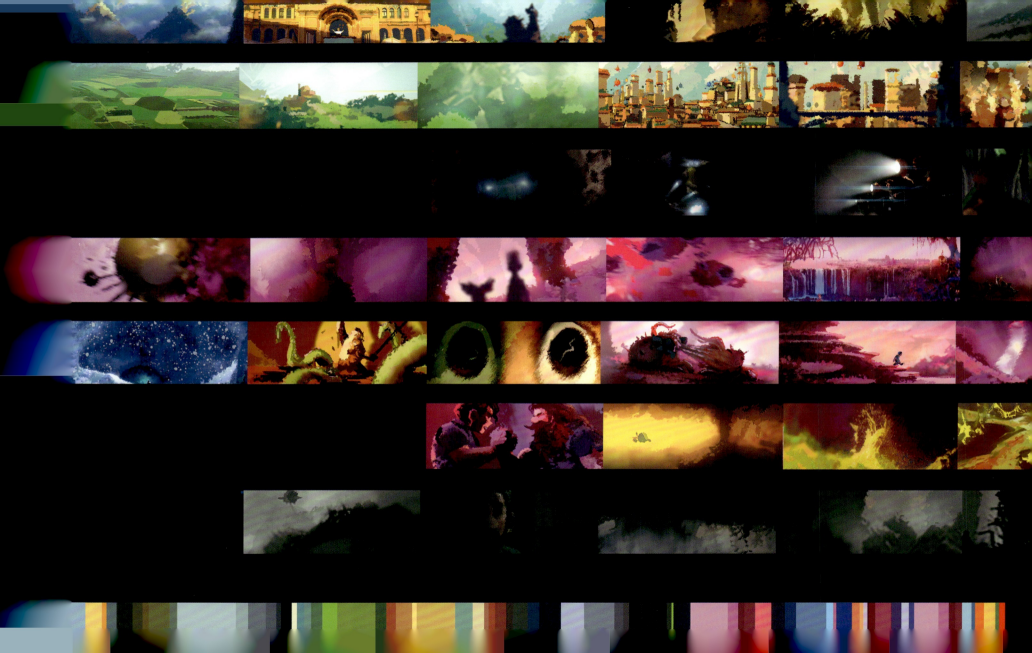

COLORSCRIPT

To establish the overall color of our film, I had to connect with the emotional arc of our characters. Each environment is a reflection of tone in the film's emotional journey. Using simple color swatches helped me organize each location and its corresponding tone. For example, the swatch for Searcher's farm was inspired by old Kodachrome images from the 1940s. Cool greens and earth tones are specific to this location. These same colors are also echoed in Searcher's clothing, connecting him to his home, the land, and his identity as a farmer.
—Justin Cram, ASSOCIATE PRODUCTION DESIGNER

THIS SPREAD Justin Cram / Digital

220 Strange World Preliminary Keys

243 Stranger in a Strange Land Preliminary Keys

261 Splat's World Preliminary Keys

In the above sequence, Searcher finds himself in a strange new world and is ultimately saved by an unknown stranger. The colors and lighting start off more saturated and lifted to emphasize a sense of Searcher's wonderment at his surroundings. Gradually, the colors become darker and higher in contrast as the world closes in and becomes a darker and scarier place. The final frame is a reveal of Jaeger, Searcher's father. The frame is staged with strong uplighting against a dark silhouette and fiery background. The audience wonders: *Is Jaeger a friend or a threat?* Color choices should always help drive the emotion.

—**Justin Cram,** ASSOCIATE PRODUCTION DESIGNER

CREATING SPLAT

Splat is a fun, gelatinous, multitentacled character inspired by a dendritic cell. In CG, we started with Jin Kim's 2D concept art. We kept Splat's flour-sack shape but pushed its limbs to feel more round, bulbous, and cartoony. Splat is one of our most imaginative characters, so much so that we've oftentimes confusingly used all sorts of anatomical terms to refer to its body parts, including arms, legs, elbows, knees, paws, belly, nubs, and nubbins.
—**Keith Wilson,** HEAD OF CHARACTERS AND TECHNICAL ANIMATION

TWIST & BEND

Jin Kim / Digital

ABOVE AND TOP Alex Kupershmidt / Digital

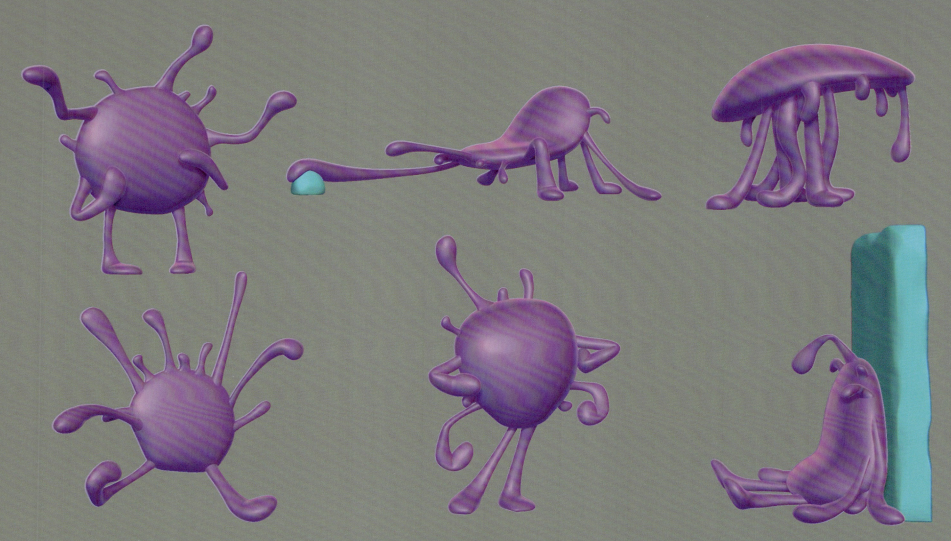

SPLAT - 3D SKETCHES

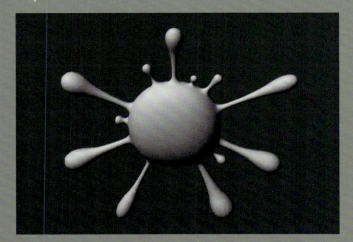

In the Modeling department, we focused on keeping Splat round. We avoided any sharp angles to make the character feel nonthreatening and friendly. Sometimes simple shapes can be challenging because they're hard to keep clean and controlled. We aimed to create a clear silhouette to preserve Splat's graphic nature.
—**Leticia TR Gillett**, CHARACTER MODEL SUPERVISOR

THIS PAGE Leticia TR Gillett / Digital

Splat's tentacles kept most of our focus in rigging. We looked at a ton of micro reference, and always keeping Splat's flowy, jelly-type movement top of mind, we improved an existing octopus character's rig by adding more bipedal mechanics so that Splat's limbs would still have tentacle-like qualities but the structure of an arm or a leg. We also created a dRig component [Disney Animation's proprietary rigging tool set] that allowed us to use it for other characters in the film, including the Reapers. Splat's unique rig has no up or down. Any appendage can be used as a leg or an arm or a "head," though Splat doesn't technically have a head! Splat is probably the most flexible (and intimidating) rig we've ever created.

—**Cameron Black**, CHARACTER TECHNICAL DIRECTOR, &
Christoffer Pedersen, CHARACTER TECHNICAL DIRECTOR

One of the things we pushed on from the beginning is that Splat shouldn't have a "right way up." We tried to avoid Splat looking too humanlike in its locomotion, and so we really wanted to play with the idea that Splat just travels in whatever way is the most fun and inventive and weird. Where a human might take a step and lean over to look at something, Splat can do half a cartwheel and end up standing on its side, and then that becomes the new "up" for that shot. Thinking about Splat that way opened up a whole series of new poses that were totally unique to Splat.

—**Justin Sklar**, HEAD OF ANIMATION

THIS PAGE Marc Bryant / Digital

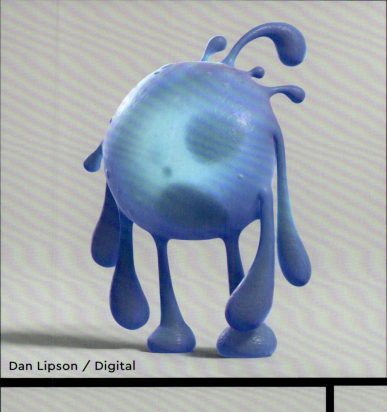

Dan Lipson / Digital

midday

overcast

morning

seq900

luna glade

acid

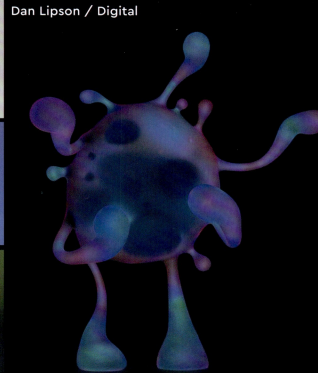

Dan Lipson / Digital

Kendall Litaker / Digital

Dan Lipson / Digital

Dan Lipson / Digital

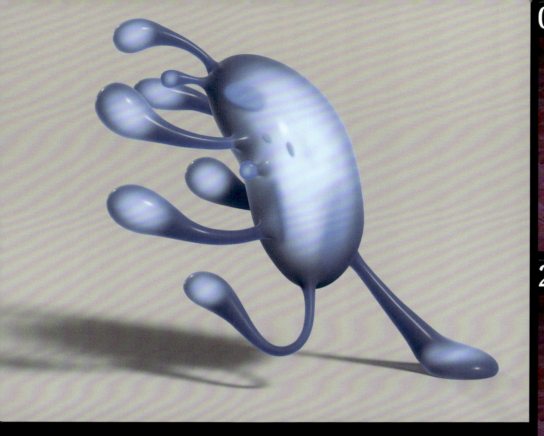

Splat's CG look and lighting development exploration went through many iterations. We looked at gummy bears, soap bubbles, and microscopic scans. We researched many different types of lighting sources, including bioluminescence. Eventually, thanks to a painting by Justin Cram, we decided Splat would glow from within and emanate "chromatic edges," or luminous color jitters of blues, greens, and purples from the surface of its form, inspired by the chromatic aberrations seen in microscopic lenses. Looking at Splat in *Strange World* is like looking at a fantastical dendritic cell under a microscope: It's believable without really making any sense! Texture-wise, Splat is a gummy bear covered in soap with some kind of volume inside.

—Dan Lipson, CHARACTER LOOK LEAD, &

Mason Khoo, CHARACTER LIGHTING LEAD

0:

1: Strongest

2: Stronger

3: Strong

4: Medium

5: Low

THIS PAGE: Mason Khoo / Digital

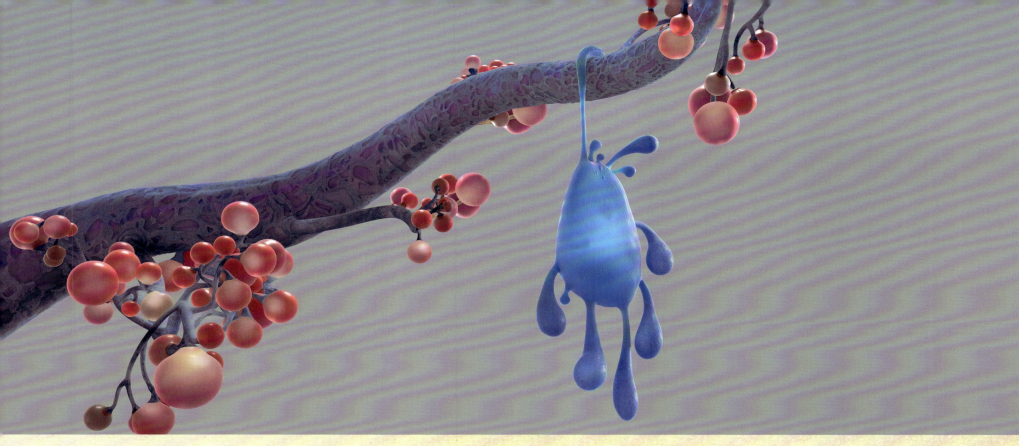

In the Lighting department, our main concern was how to make the non-photorealistically shaded Splat, who is lit from within and whom light passes through, feel like it was believably in an environment. The key was controlling Splat's chromatic edge to give a feeling that it was responding to the external lighting in the way it should, similarly to how an audience knows a piece of wood or dirt should respond when lit. Early effects animation exploration by [Effects Supervisor] Marc Bryant and later collaboration with the technology team—[Senior Engineer, Software] Wei-Feng Wayne Huang, [Principal Engineer, Software] Brent Burley, [Senior Engineer, Software] Matt Jen-Yuan Chiang, [Associate Technical Supervisor] Kendall Litaker, and [Technical Supervisor] Mark Hammel—helped us develop an efficient shading and rendering system to achieve the vision of [Character Look Lead] Dan Lipson and [Character Lighting Lead] Mason Khoo's Splat development work. The result is a character that responds to light differently than any other character in Disney Animation's history.
—**Brian Leach**, DIRECTOR OF CINEMATOGRAPHY, LIGHTING

THIS PAGE
Various Artists / Digital

167

BUILDING A STRANGE WORLD

220/8 & 8.7
Set dressing drawover for
Foregrouund platforms

Waterfalls ?

Building our lively and complex CG Windy Jungle environment required a great deal of innovation and collaboration among many departments, including Layout, Modeling, Look, Lighting, Set Extension, and Effects Animation.

We began our process by studying storyboards of sequences shot in the Windy Jungle. The storyboards showed long panning shots of the whole environment, so we had to map out the entire set. The top image shows our first mapping attempt. The second is a refinement of the first, created after Layout played with camera positioning in the set. We also used this sketch to communicate set dressing, which is the process of adding plants and other elements to the scene to make it complete.

To the right is a foundation lighting pass, an early step taken by Lighting to establish what a scene will look like so that all departments can plan for the lighting situation. This pass also helped us see how the whole shot would come together

Scout Model

Final Model

Look Development

Set Extension

Modeling began by making a library of plants and environment pieces that were later used to create the set. We made a ton of plant life that can be seen all over the Windy Jungle, from the Pop Trees and ground cover to the giant platforms. All these pieces were added to the set to create a rough pass scout model, as shown in the image to the left.

Layout then went into the scout model to figure out shots and cameras. At the same time, Modeling continued their work, defining surfaces and detailing out all the geometry used in the set. The higher-resolution ground planes and environmental elements that the characters would be interacting with were passed on to Animation so they could begin animating.

Next in the pipeline was Look development, which added texture and material details to our library of plant models. They also created a library of smaller details using Disney's XGen tool in Maya that could be added to a set, such as grasses. To help animation, Look then took a pass on surfaces where characters would be moving. Look development artists worked closely with Lighting the entire time to ensure that the materials in the set were responding to light in the right way.

Set Extension is the final department of the Environments team. Early on, they created rough backgrounds and landscapes that the other departments used to see what the final scene would look like. The image to the left shows a work-in-progress set extension. Set extension artists also worked closely with Lighting so the sky and backgrounds established the feeling and look the Lighting team aimed to achieve.

The last secret that brought the environment to life was the Effects Animation team. Responsible for creating movement for all plant life within the set, Effects also innovated new processes that allowed upstream departments, such as Set Dressing and Look, to work with already-animated assets. Thanks to Effects, our typical smoke plumes and atmospherics appeared with unusual characteristics that gave us extra richness and pushed the strangeness of the Windy Jungle.

—**Charles Cunningham-Scott**, ENVIRONMENT MODELING SUPERVISOR;
Ben Fiske, ANIMATED ENVIRONMENTS SUPERVISOR; **Logan Gloor**, ENVIRONMENT LIGHTING LEAD; **Sean D. Jenkins**, HEAD OF ENVIRONMENTS; **Michael Kaschalk**, HEAD OF EFFECTS; **Brian Leach**, DIRECTOR OF CINEMATOGRAPHY, LIGHTING; **Adil Mustafabekov**, SET EXTENSIONS SUPERVISOR; & **Lance Summers**, ENVIRONMENT LOOK SUPERVISOR

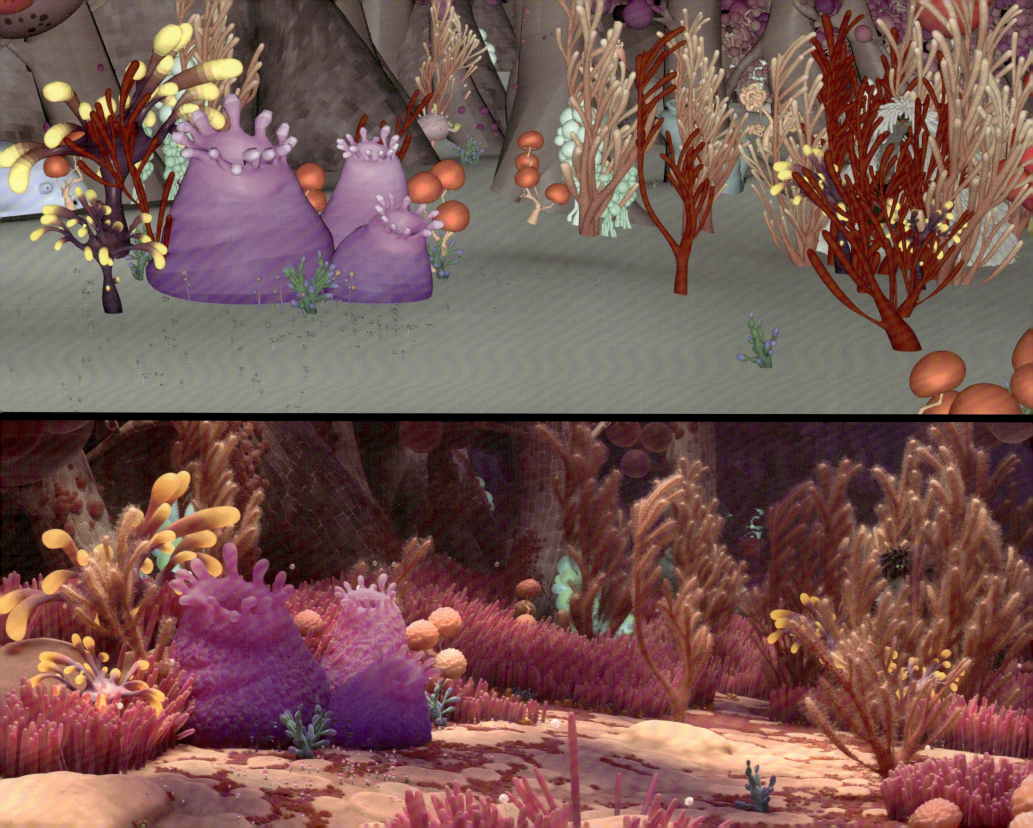

THIS SPREAD Various Artists / Digital

Cinematography

With so much to do and see in *Strange World*, we all knew from the very beginning that only a widescreen aspect ratio, 2.39:1, would do justice for our adventure film.

We designed our camera choices to contrast our two very different worlds. In Avalonia, for example, we shot scenes with spherical lenses, the assumed type for feature films, to give a nostalgic quality to them. To contrast scenes in the Strange World, we used less typical, oval-shaped anamorphic lenses to take advantage of the unusual effects they produced, such as stretched bokeh, flares, and other types of lens distortions.

Searcher's character arc also drove our camera choices. His happy moments were paired with high saturation and his low moments with desaturation. To romanticize his beloved farm, we utilized shallow depth of field to focus in on the same details that Searcher found beautiful, as if the audience were looking at the world through his eyes. We also created two types of compositions—"united" and "divided"—to show connectedness or separation between Searcher and other characters. In a united composition, we used a longer lens, which allowed us to flatten out the background and focus on the characters in the foreground to give a feeling of togetherness. In a divided composition, we used a wider lens to spread characters apart to give a feeling of separateness.

Given that there is no light source in the Strange World, we had to invent a way to bring light in. We aimed for a "natural-but-ambiguous" look and found creative ways to bring light in, including through bioluminescence. In addition, adding a bright fog to the horizon helped create that feeling reminiscent of a sunrise or sunset on an overcast day.

—**Scott Beattie,** DIRECTOR OF CINEMATOGRAPHY, LAYOUT, & **Brian Leach,** DIRECTOR OF CINEMATOGRAPHY, LIGHTING

THIS SPREAD Various Artists / Digital

ACKNOWLEDGMENTS

We both have a special love for *Strange World*, as we've both had the pleasure of working on the film from its creative development and cultural standpoints. It has been a true privilege to work on this special book that celebrates the film's extraordinary art. Thank you, Don Hall, Qui Nguyen, and Roy Conli, for allowing us to be a part of this journey!

Thank you to Mehrdad Isvandi, Justin Cram, Jin Kim, Larry Wu, Lissa Treiman, David G. Derrick Jr., and the many artists who helped build this book. The world is a better place because of your art.

We could not have created this book without the amazing Kelly Eisert and Natalia Adame Mendoza. Thanks to John I. McGuire, Christine M. Neuharth, Shirley Scopelitis, Gus Avila, Amy Astley, Erin Glover, Danielle Song, Peter Del Vecho, Jessica Julius, Brandy Fisher, and Dr. S. Steve Arounsack for your partnership and support. Laurie Au, Kristin Leigh Yadamec, and Jenna Hascher, thank you for leading the way.

Thank you to the incredible team at Chronicle Books—Maddy Wong, Brittany McInerney, Jon H. Glick, and Neil Egan—for your hard work and artistry bringing these stunning books to life. To the Disney Publishing dream team, Alison Giordano, Andi Cochrane, and Jackson Kaplan, thank you for the many hours you spent with us to make sure this book turned out just right. We really love working with you!

A note from Juan Pablo: Thank you to my family, my mom, siblings, in-laws, nieces, and nephews. But particularly to my dad, Jaime, for being such a great role model. You've been in my mind throughout this process, writing a book and working on a project about fathers and sons. I love you. I would also like to thank my husband Christopher, (MDA). What a special moment this is for us to see a character like us on the page and on the screen!

A note from Kaliko: Thank you to my dad, Tim, the ultimate Kanaka Maoli man and our family's unsung hero. Kamalani (Mom), Kawehi, Kaleo, and I love you so much. And to Chase, thank you for adventuring through this life with me.

Best wishes,
Kaliko and Juan Pablo